SHARING JESUS

6 SMALL GROUP SESSIONS ON EVANGELISM

STUDENT EDITION

DOUG FIELDS & BRETT EASTMAN

ZONDERVAN™

GRAND RAPIDS, MICHIGAN 49530 USA

ZONDERVAN.COM/
AUTHORTRACKER

Youth Specialties
www.youthspecialties.com

Youth Specialties

Sharing Jesus, Student Edition: Six Sessions on Evangelism
Copyright © 2006 by Doug Fields and Brett Eastman

Youth Specialties products, 300 South Pierce Street, El Cajon, CA 92020,
are published by Zondervan, 5300 Patterson Avenue SE, Grand Rapids,
MI 49530

Library of Congress Cataloging-in-Publication Data

Fields, Doug, 1962-
  Sharing Jesus : 6 small group sessions on evangelism / Doug Fields and
Brett Eastman.
    p. cm. -- (Experiencing Christ together, student edition)
  ISBN-10: 0-310-26648-3 (pbk.)
  ISBN-13: 978-0-310-26648-8 (pbk.)
  1. Witness bearing (Christianity)--Biblical teaching. 2. Evangelistic work-
-Biblical teaching. 3. Witness bearing--Study and teaching. 4. Evangelistic
work--Study and teaching. I. Eastman, Brett, 1959- II. Title.

BV4520.F52 2006
268'.433--dc22

                                                                2005024176

*Creative Team: Dave Urbanski, Holly Sharp, Mark Novelli, Joanne Heim,
Janie Wilkerson*
Cover Design: Mattson Creative
Printed in the United States of America

05 06 07 08 09 10 • 10 9 8 7 6 5 4 3 2 1

ACKNOWLEDGMENTS

This series of six books couldn't have happened if there weren't some wonderful friends who chimed in on the process and added their heart and level of expertise to these pages. I need to acknowledge and thank my friends for loving God, caring for students and supporting me-especially true on this task were Amanda Maguire, Nancy Varner, Ryanne Dearden, Jana Sarti, Matt McGill and the crew at Simply Youth Ministry. I sure appreciate doing life together. Also, I'm very appreciative of Brett Eastman for asking me to do this project.

TABLE OF CONTENTS

INTRODUCTION: READ ME FIRST!

Welcome to a Journey with Jesus (and Others)!

I hope you're ready for God to do something great in your life as you use this book and connect with a few friends and a loving small group leader. The potential of this combination is incredible. The reason we know its potential is because we've heard from thousands of students who've already gone through our first series of LIFETOGETHER books and shared their stories. We've been blessed to hear that the combination of friends gathering together, books with great questions, and the Bible as a foundation have provided the ingredients for life change. As you read these words, know that you're beginning a journey that may revolutionize your life.

The following six sessions are designed to help you grow in your knowledge of Jesus and his teachings and become his devoted disciple. But growth doesn't happen alone. You need God's help and a community of people who love God, too. We've found that a great way to grow strong in Christ is in the context of a caring, spiritual community (or small group). This community is committed to doing life together—at least for a season—and will thrive when each small group member (you) focuses on Jesus as well as the others in the group.

This type of spiritual community isn't easy. It requires several things from you:

- trust
- confidentiality
- honesty
- care
- openness
- risk
- commitment to meet regularly

Anyone can meet with a few people and call it a "group," but it takes stronger commitment and desire to create a spiritual community where others can know you, love you, care for you, and give you the freedom to open up about your thoughts, doubts, and struggles—a place where you're safe to be yourself.

We've learned from the small groups that didn't work that spiritual community can't develop without honesty. Now, at first you may be tempted to show up to your small group session and sit, smile, act nicely, and never speak from your heart—but this type of superficial participation prevents true spiritual community. Please fight through this temptation and know that when you reveal who you really are, you'll contribute something unique and powerful to the group that can't occur any other way. Your honest sharing about your heart and soul will challenge other group members to do the same, and they'll likely become as honest as you are.

To help you get to this place of honesty, every session contains questions that are intended to push you to think, talk, and open your heart. They'll challenge you to expose some of your fears, hurts, and habits. Through them, I guarantee you'll experience spiritual growth and relational intimacy, and you'll build lasting, genuine friendships.

All mature Christians will tell you that God used others to impact their lives. God has a way of allowing one life to connect with another to result in richer, deeper, and more vibrant lives for both. As you go through this book (and the five others in this series), you will have the opportunity to impact someone else—and someone else will have the opportunity to impact you. You'll both become deeper, stronger followers of Jesus Christ. So get ready for some life change.

WHO IS JESUS?

Most people have an opinion about Jesus. But many of these opinions are based on what they've heard or come up with on their own—what they'd *prefer* Jesus to be—as opposed to their own discovery of Jesus through the Bible. People believe Jesus was all kinds of things—a great teacher, a leader of a revolution, a radical with a political agenda, a gentle man with a big vision, a prophet, a spiritual person who emphasized religion. Still others believe he is who he claimed to be—God.

The Jesus of the Bible is far more compelling than most people's opinions about him. *Sharing Jesus* allows you to get to know Jesus as his first followers did. They met Jesus as Teacher, a rabbi. They came to know Jesus as Healer, Shepherd, Servant, Savior, and ultimately the One who defeated death—the risen Lord. From his first words, "Follow me," through his ministry, death, and resurrection, he kept drawing people deeper into his life.

Jesus asked his disciples to commit their lives to God's way. As you read the Bible, you'll see that God's ways weren't always easy or comfortable for the disciples to follow. But what motivated them to do what he taught was their rich experience of who he was and all he did for them. *Sharing Jesus* will ground you in that same experience so you'll more fully desire to follow Jesus and commit to his ways—even when it's not easy or comfortable. The Jesus you're about to encounter is waiting for you to meet him, get closer to him, and commit your life to following his ways and teachings.

When you align your life with Jesus, you're in for a wild, adventurous life. It won't be without its difficulties, but it'll be a better life than you ever dreamed possible.

WHAT YOU NEED TO KNOW ABOUT EACH OF THESE SIX SESSIONS

Each session in this study contains more material than you and your group can complete in a typical meeting of an hour or so. The key to making the most of each session is to choose which questions you'll answer and discuss and which ones you'll save for your alone time. We've tried to make it simple, so if you miss something from one meeting, you can pick it up the next time you're together. Let's be more specific.

Each of the six sessions in *Sharing Jesus* contains five unique sections. These five sections have the same titles in every book and in every session in the LIFETOGETHER series. The sections are (1) fellowship, (2) discipleship, (3) ministry, (4) evangelism, and (5) worship. These represent five biblical purposes that we believe lead to personal spiritual growth, growth in your student ministry, and health for your entire church. The more you think about these five purposes and try to make them part of your life, the stronger you'll be and the more you'll grow spiritually.

While these five biblical purposes make sense individually, they can make a greater impact when they're brought together. Think of it in sports terms: If you play baseball or softball, you might be an outstanding hitter—but you also need to catch, throw, run, and slide. You need more than one skill to impact your team. In the same way, having a handle on one or two of the five biblical purposes is great—but when they're all reflected together in a person's life, that person is much more biblically balanced and healthy.

You'll find that the material in this book (and in the other LIFETOGETHER books) is built around the Bible. There are a lot of blank spaces and journaling pages where you can write down your thoughts about God's Word and God's work in your life as you explore and live out God's biblical purposes.

Each session begins with a short story that helps introduce the theme. If you have time to read it, great—if not, no big deal. Immediately following the story are five key sections. The following is a brief description of each:

♥ FELLOWSHIP: CONNECTING YOUR HEART TO OTHERS

Goal: To share about your life and listen attentively to others, caring about what they share

You'll begin your session with a few minutes of conversation that will give you all a chance to share from your own lives, get to know each other better, and offer initial thoughts about the session's theme. The icon for this section is a heart because you're opening up your heart so others can connect with you on a deeper level.

DISCIPLESHIP: GROWING TO BE LIKE JESUS

Goal: To explore God's Word, gain biblical knowledge, and make personal applications

This section will take the most time. You'll explore the Bible and gain some knowledge about Jesus. You'll encounter his life and teachings and discuss how God's Word can make a difference in your own life. The icon for this section is a brain because you're opening your mind to learn God's Word and his ways.

You'll find lots of questions in this section—more than you can discuss during your group time. Your leader will choose the questions you have time to discuss or come up with different questions. We encourage you to respond to the skipped questions on your own; during the week it's a great way to get more Bible study time.

MINISTRY: SERVING OTHERS IN LOVE

Goal: To recognize and take advantage of opportunities to serve others

When you get to this section, you'll have an opportunity to discuss how to express God's love through serving others. The discussion and opportunities are created to tie into the topic. As you grow spiritually, you'll naturally begin to recognize and take opportunities to serve others. As your heart grows, so will your opportunities to serve. Here, the icon is a foot because feet communicate movement and action—serving and meeting the needs of others requires you to act on what you've learned.

EVANGELISM: SHARING YOUR STORY AND GOD'S STORY

Goal: To consider how the truths from this session might be applied to your relationships with unbelievers

It's very easy for a small group to turn into a clique that only looks inward and loses sight of others outside the group. That's not God's plan. God wants you to reach out to people with his message of love and life change. While this is often scary, this section will give you an opportunity to discuss your relationships with non-Christians and consider ways to listen to their stories, share pieces of your story, and reflect the amazing love of God's story. The icon for this section is a mouth because you're opening your mouth to have spiritual conversations with nonbelievers.

WORSHIP: SURRENDERING YOUR LIFE TO HONOR GOD

Goal: To focus on God's presence

Each session ends with a time of prayer. You'll be challenged to slow down and turn your focus toward God's love, his goodness, and his presence in your life. You'll spend time talking to God, listening in silence, reading Scripture, writing, and focusing on God. The key word for this time is *surrender*, which is giving up what you want so God can give you what he wants. The icon for this section is a body, which represents surrendering your entire life to God.

Oh yeah…there are more sections in each session!

In addition to the main material, there are several additional options you can use to help further and deepen your times with God. Many people attend church programs, listen, and then "leave" God until the next week when they return to church. We don't want that to happen to you! So we've provided several more opportunities for you to learn, reflect, and grow on your own.

At the end of every session you'll find three more key headings:

- At Home This Week
- Learn a Little More
- For Deeper Study on Your Own

They're fairly easy to figure out, but here's a brief description of each:

AT HOME THIS WEEK

There are five options presented at the end of each session that you can do on your own. They're not homework for the next session (unless your leader assigns them to your group); they're things you can do to keep growing at your own pace. You can skip them, you can do all of them, or you can vary the options from session to session.

Option 1: A Weekly Reflection

At the end of each session you'll find a one-page, quick self-evaluation that helps you reflect on the five key areas of your spiritual life (fellowship, discipleship, ministry, evangelism, and worship). It's simply a guide for you to gauge your spiritual health. The first one is on page 29.

Option 2: Daily Bible Readings

One of the challenges in deepening your knowledge of God's Word and learning more about Jesus' life is to read the Bible on your own. This option provides a guide to help you read through some of Paul's writings in 36 days. On pages 114-115 is a list of Bible passages to help you continue to take God's Word deeper into your life.

Option 3: Memory Verses

On pages 119-120 you'll find six Bible verses to memorize. Each is related to the theme of a particular session. (Again, these are optional...remember, nothing is mandatory!)

Option 4: Journaling

You'll find a question or two related to the theme of the session that can serve as a trigger to get you writing. Journaling is a great way to reflect on what you've been learning and evaluate your life. In addition to questions at the end of each session, there's a helpful tool on pages 121-123 that can guide you through the discipline of journaling.

Option 5: Wrap It Up

As you've already read, each session contains too many questions for one small group meeting. So this section provides opportunities to think through your answers to the questions you skipped and then go back and write them down.

LEARN A LITTLE MORE

We've provided some insights (or commentary) on some of the passages that you'll study to help you understand the difficult terms, phrases, and people that you'll read about in each Bible passage.

FOR DEEPER STUDY ON YOUR OWN

One of the best ways to understand the Bible passages and the theme of each session is to dig a little deeper. If deeper study fits your personality style, please use these additional ideas as ways to enhance your learning.

WHAT YOU NEED TO KNOW ABOUT BEING IN A SMALL GROUP

You probably have enough casual or superficial friendships and don't need to waste your time cultivating more. We all need deep and committed friendships. Here are a few ideas to help you benefit the most from your small group time and build great relationships.

Prepare to Participate

Interaction is a key to a good small group. Talking too little will make it hard for others to get to know you. Everyone has something to contribute—yes, even you! But participating doesn't mean dominating, so be careful to not monopolize the conversation. Most groups typically have one conversation hog, and if you don't know who it is in your small group, then it might be you. Here's a tip: You don't have to answer every question and comment on every point. Try to find a balance between the two extremes.

Be Consistent

Healthy relationships take time to grow. Quality time is great, but a great quantity of time is probably better. Commit with your group to show up every week (or whenever your group plans to meet), even when you don't feel like it. With only six sessions per book, if you miss just two meetings you'll have missed a third of what's presented in these pages. When you make a commitment to your small group a high priority, you're sure to build meaningful relationships.

Practice Honesty and Confidentiality

Strong relationships are only as solid as the trust they are built upon. Although it may be difficult, take a risk and be honest with your answers. God wants you to be known by others! Then respect the risks others are taking and offer them the same love, grace, and forgiveness God does. Make confidentiality a nonnegotiable value for your small group. Nothing kills community like gossip.

Arrive Ready to Grow

You can always arrive prepared by praying ahead of time. Ask God to give you the courage to be honest and the discipline to respect others.

You aren't required to do any preparation in the book before you arrive (unless you're the leader—see page 88). If your leader chooses to, she may ask you to do the Discipleship

**Doug Fields &
Brett Eastman**

Doug and Brett were
part of the same small
group for several
years. Brett was the
pastor of small groups
at Saddleback Church
where Doug is the
pastor to students.
Brett and a team of
friends wrote DOING
LIFETOGETHER,
a group study for
adults. Everyone
loved it so much that
they asked Doug to
take the same theme
and Bible verses
and revise the other
material for students.
So even though Brett
and Doug both had
a hand in writing
this book, the book
you're using is written
by Doug—and as a
youth pastor, he's
cheering you on in
your small group
experience. For more
information on Doug
and Brett see page
144.

section ahead of time so that you'll have more time to discuss the other sections and make better use of your time.

Congratulations...

...for making a commitment to go through this material with your small group! Life change is within reach when people are united through the same commitment. Your participation in a small group can have a lasting and powerful impact on your life. Our prayer is that the questions and activities in this book help you grow closer to the other group members, and more importantly, to God.

If you're a small group leader, please turn to page 89 for a brief instruction on how to best use this material.

SMALL GROUP COVENANT

One of the signs of a healthy small group is that all members understand its purpose. We've learned that members of good small groups make a bond, a commitment, or a covenant to one another.

Read through the following covenant as a group. Be sure to discuss your concerns and questions before you begin your first session. Please feel free to modify the covenant based on the needs and concerns of your particular group. Once you agree with the terms and are willing to commit to the covenant (as you've revised it), sign your own book and have the others sign yours.

With a covenant, your entire group will have the same purpose for your time together, allowing you to grow together and go deeper into your study of God's Word. Without a covenant, groups often find themselves meeting simply for the sake of meeting.

If your group decides to add some additional values, write them at the bottom of the covenant page. Your group may also want to create some rules (such as not interrupting when someone else is speaking or sitting up instead of lying down). You can list those at the bottom of the covenant page also.

Reviewing your group's covenant, values, and rules before each meeting can become a significant part of your small group experience.

A covenant is a binding agreement or contract. God made covenants with Noah, Abraham, and David, among others. Jesus is the fulfillment of a new covenant between God and his people.

SMALL GROUP COVENANT

I, _____, as a member of our small group, acknowledge my need for meaningful relationships with other believers. I agree that this small group community exists to help me deepen my relationships with God, Christians, and other people in my life. I commit to the following:

Consistency

I will give my best effort to attend each of our group meetings.

Honesty

I will take risks to share truthfully about the personal issues in my life.

Confidentiality

I will support the foundation of trust in our small group by not participating in gossip. I will not reveal personal information shared by others during our meetings.

Respect

I will help create a safe environment for our small group members by listening carefully and not making fun of others.

Prayer

I commit to pray regularly for the people in our small group.

Accountability

I will allow the people in my small group to hold me accountable for growing spiritually and living a life that honors God.

This covenant, signed by all the members in this group, reflects our commitment to one another.

Date:

Names:

Additional values our small group members agree to

Additional rules our small group members agree to

THE FATHER'S HEART

⭐ **LEADERS, READ PAGE 88.**

Jake could hardly believe it.

The television program he was watching suddenly became one of those "we interrupt this program…" breaking-news stories. It was the day after Christmas, and a tidal wave (also known as a tsunami) had hit the coasts of Sri Lanka and Indonesia in Southeast Asia. Initial reports said that tens of thousands had died.

Despite the television imagery, Jake could barely comprehend a number so large. He wondered what the damage and devastation would mean for this poverty-stricken country. (In the end, more than 300,000 people were killed by the tsunami.)

The following week, Jake shared his feelings and concerns with his small group—he just couldn't shake those images of humans in need. The group began praying for the people and families experiencing tragedy. Even though the small group of teenage guys were thousands of miles away and didn't know anyone personally involved in the crisis, their hearts were breaking over the pain they saw on television. The group began to view the people of Southeast Asia through God's eyes and discuss how pained God must feel when his people hurt.

But the guys didn't just talk about the pain; they sent money and care packages as often as they could. That summer they went on a mission trip with their church to Sri Lanka to help those who needed assistance. Not only were they helping people in a horrible situation, but their hearts were changing as well.

Amazing things happen when we allow ourselves to feel for people the way God must feel when he sees them in need. That's what this session is all about—developing a tender heart for others. *More specifically, it's about developing a heart for those who don't know God.* The word for this is *evangelism.* God wants evangelism to well up within us as our hearts become more like his. Just as compassion for the lost gripped Christ and motivated his action, the same concern for those living without God ought to compel us to action as well.

♥ FELLOWSHIP: CONNECTING YOUR HEART TO OTHERS

Goal: To share about your life and listen attentively to others, caring about what they share

Just a reminder: There probably isn't enough time in your small-group session to answer every question. Instead choose which ones you'll answer, and then answer the others on your own time. Have fun!

If you're new to this series of books, you'll find that every time you get to the fellowship section, the questions are designed to get you talking and knowing each other better. If you're a veteran of the series (which means that you've been through some of the other books), then you already know what to do.

Answer one of these two questions:

1. If you're a Christian, what was your life like before you had a personal relationship with God? What did you know about Jesus? What did you think about Jesus?

What did you think about people who claimed to have a relationship with Jesus?

2. Think of one person in your life who doesn't know Jesus. Briefly describe your relationship with that person. (Is that person a family member, a close friend, or a neighbor?) How do you feel about him or her not knowing Jesus?

If your group hasn't discussed the small group covenant on page 18, please take some time now to go through it. Make commitments to each other that your group time will reflect those values (and any additional ones you add). One sign of a healthy small group is that it begins each session by reading the covenant together as a constant reminder of what the group has committed to.

 ## DISCIPLESHIP: GROWING TO BE LIKE JESUS

Goal: To explore God's Word, gain biblical knowledge, and make personal applications

It's easy to get comfortable in life. Seeking comfort isn't necessarily a bad thing. You wouldn't deliberately wear shoes that were too small just so you could feel pain, right? Comfort in friendships isn't bad, either. Without comfort, every conversation would be difficult and shallow, filled with awkward pauses and insecurity. It's good to have a safe place with friends who provide support, encouragement, and fun.

But comfort can become dangerous when it blinds our eyes to others' needs. Too much comfort can come at the expense of those who may need your compassion. As you study this passage, see if you can discover what's important to God.

Read Luke 15:1-10. (If you don't have a Bible, the passage is on page 93.)

1. What situation prompted Jesus to tell the stories (also called *parables*) about the lost sheep and coin?

2. Why do you think the Pharisees were so critical of Jesus?

3. Since Jesus hung out with the tax collectors and "sinners," does that mean Christians can hang out with whomever they want—no matter what? Why, or why not?

4. What do these parables teach about God's character?

5. When do you find it easy to judge others? What qualities or actions do you look down upon?

6. Read verse 7 again. Does it mean that God and the angels care more about non-Christians who cry for help than Christians who remain strong in their faith? Explain your answer.

7. What role does joy play in these parables? How can this motivate us? How does joy play out in the lives of the Pharisees and teachers of the law?

8. In your opinion, what is the best way to help someone come to repentance?

9. Which of the following best describes a picture of your spiritual life right now? Explain your answer.

   a. A tax collector in need of repentance
   b. A Pharisee, judging the lost and those who are trying to help them
   c. A disciple, trying to reach out to the lost

EVANGELISM: SHARING YOUR STORY AND GOD'S STORY

Goal: To consider how the truths from this session might be applied to your relationships with unbelievers

We have found that time alone with God is essential for developing a heart for the lost (those separated from God). The Bible is full of ideas about how to pray for our friends—and for ourselves! (See Colossians 4:2-6 for one example.) In prayer we can tell God our fears regarding evangelism, our frustrations that others aren't coming to faith in Jesus, and our dreams for our lost friends.

We hope you'll make it your goal over the next six weeks to develop your heart for the lost by praying for them. Prayer will stretch your heart and make you sensitive to those who live their lives without God.

1. Think about family members, neighbors, and friends who may not know God. Write at least three or four names below. (These names are private—they're just for *your* prayer life.)

2. Commit to praying for these people throughout this study, both with your group and on your own. Ask God to show you his heart for them.

3. Ask God to make you a person of prayer—someone who is sensitive to the needs of others and the spiritual condition of those around you.

For the health of your small group, be sure to read the clique section on pages 103-104. It's vital for your group to decide at this first session whether you can invite friends to join your group. Talk about the structure of your group and stick to your decision. If you decide the answer is no, you may be able to invite friends to join you in the next EXPERIENCING CHRIST TOGETHER book—there are six of them, so there's plenty of time! If you're a small-group leader, see the Small Group Leader Checklist on page 88.

MINISTRY: SERVING OTHERS IN LOVE

Goal: To recognize and take advantage of opportunities to serve others

One of the ways you can have a ministry to others (especially those in your group) is to provide personal accountability. It's easy to talk about evangelism and list friends who don't know Jesus, but it's difficult to care for those friends.

It is especially difficult to find time to listen to a friend's personal story and learn more about her. The goal of this six-session book isn't simply to study evangelism, it's to practice it and develop an evangelistic mindset that will inspire you to care for people and listen to their stories with the hope of having opportunities to share your faith story and then point them to *God's* amazing love story.

To do this, it's good to have help and accountability—that's one of the benefits of being in a small group.

1. Find one other person in your group to be your "accountability partner" during this study. A partner's job isn't to nag; it's to encourage you to develop a heart for the lost. Take a minute to identify this person in your group. Write down how you'll hold each other accountable.

2. Take one minute to discuss the role of an accountability partner. You'll have other opportunities throughout this book to discuss topics that relate to your life and evangelism.

WORSHIP: SURRENDERING YOUR LIFE TO HONOR GOD

Goal: To focus on God's presence

Prayer connects our hearts with God's heart for the lost. God wants us to ask him to do things that reflect his heart and connect our hearts to his ways. Make sure you save time at the end of each session to pray together.

1. Look at the names you listed on page 23. Below, write down exactly what you're praying will happen to this person or these people. (In other words, if God answers your exact prayer, what would each of their lives look like?)

You'll find three prayer resources in the appendices in the back of this book. By reading them (and possibly discussing them), you'll find your group prayer time more rewarding.
• Praying in Your Small Group (pages 130-131). Read this article on your own before the next session.
• Prayer Request Guidelines (pages 132-133). Read and discuss these guidelines as a group.
• Prayer Options (pages 134-135). Refer to this list for ideas to add variety to your prayer time.

2. Pray silently for the names on your list.

3. Close in prayer as a group and ask God to give each of you a heart like his—a heart that cares for those who are separated from him.

AT HOME THIS WEEK

One of the consistent values of our LIFETOGETHER books is that we want you to have options for growing spiritually on your own during the week. To help with this "on your own" value, we'll give you five options. If you do these, you'll have more to contribute when you return to your small group, and you'll begin to develop spiritual habits that can last your entire life. Here are the five you'll see after every section. (You might try to do one per day on the days after your small group meets.)

Option 1: A Weekly Reflection

After each session you'll find a quick, one-page self-evaluation that reflects the five areas of your spiritual life found in this book (fellowship, discipleship, ministry, evangelism, and worship). After each evaluation, you decide if there's anything you'll do differently with your life. This page is all for *you*. It's not intended as a report card that you turn into your small group leader. The first evaluation is on pages 30-31.

Option 2: Daily Bible Readings

On pages 114-115 you'll find a list of Bible passages that will help you read through an entire section of the Bible in 30 days. If you choose this option, try to read one of the assigned passages each day. Highlight key verses in your Bible, reflect on them, journal about them, or write down any questions you have from your reading. We want to encourage you to take time to read God's love letter—the Bible. You'll find helpful tips in "How to Study the Bible on Your Own" (pages 116-118).

Option 3: Memory Verses

Memorizing Bible verses is an important habit to develop as you learn to grow spiritually on your own. "Memory Verses" (pages 119-120) contains six verses for you to memorize—one per session. Memorizing verses (and making them stick for more than a few minutes) isn't easy, but the benefits are undeniable. You'll have God's Word with you wherever you go.

"I HAVE HIDDEN YOUR WORD IN MY HEART THAT I MIGHT NOT SIN AGAINST YOU." —PSALM 119:11

Option 4: Journaling

You'll find blank pages for journaling beginning on page 124. At the end of each session, you'll find questions to get your thoughts going—but you aren't limited to answering the questions listed. Use these pages to reflect, write a letter to God, note what you're learning, compose prayer, ask questions, draw pictures, record your thoughts, or take notes if your small group is using the EXPERIENCING CHRIST TOGETHER DVD teachings. For some suggestions about journaling, turn to "Journaling: Snapshot of Your Heart" on page 121.

For this session, choose one or more questions to kickstart your journaling.

- I'm excited to be in a group because...
- If someone asked me to describe Jesus, I would say...
- Jesus would want me to know...

Option 5: Wrap It Up

Write out your answers to any questions that you didn't answer during your small group time.

Of the five options listed here, mark the option(s) that seem most appealing to you. Share with your group the one(s) you plan to do in the upcoming week. This helps you keep one another accountable as you continue to study and grow on your own.

LEARN A LITTLE MORE

Goal: To help you better understand the Scripture passage you studied in this session by highlighting key words and other important information.

Tax collectors (Luke 15:1)

No one has ever enjoyed paying taxes—but in Jesus' day, the Jewish people considered their tax collectors to be "sinners." Why? Because they were typically fellow Jews who worked for the Roman government that occupied Israel in the first century A.D. What's more, they were permitted to collect more taxes than the Romans required—and to keep the extra money for themselves. The Jewish people viewed tax collectors as corrupt traitors. As a result, the religious leaders wanted nothing to do with them. Then along came Jesus, who blew everyone away when he chose to hang out with tax collectors (even one of his 12 disciples—Matthew—was a tax collector). This is especially significant to the meaning of this passage concerning those who sin against others.

Pharisees (15:2)

In Jesus' day, the Pharisees were a powerful group of religious leaders. They sought to bring the Word of God to the people in their homes, rather than in the temple through worship. They viewed the entire Old Testament as inspired directly from God (not all Jewish groups believed this). Pharisees also considered the oral tradition (teachings passed down from generation to generation) to be just as authoritative as the rest of the Old Testament. In the Gospels, the Pharisees are almost always seen negatively: "...their piety is attacked as hypocritical, their spiritual leadership is declared bankrupt, and they are charged with leading the nation to its doom."[1]

Teachers of the Law (15:2)

Teachers of the law were sometimes called "scribes." Scribes played an important role in the Jewish faith—they were responsible for copying and preserving both Scripture and the

[1]Green, J. B., McKnight, S., & Marshall, I. H, *Dictionary of Jesus and the Gospels.* (Downers Grove, Ill.: InterVarsity Press, 1992), page 609.

teachings of the rabbis (or teachers). Scribes were also considered authoritative teachers due to their familiarity with the Law of Moses. Based on their portrayal in the Gospels, they are probably "best understood as bureaucrats and experts on Jewish life."[2]

Sinners (15:1-2)

The teachers of the law had traditions that spelled out exactly how to live in obedience to God's law. Their intentions were admirable, but the traditions made it impossible for people to live in complete obedience. Why? For instance, shepherds were classified as "impure" because they handled dead animals and couldn't afford to pay for cleansing rituals. And tax collecting was as on the same level as prostitution. Yet Jesus spent his time among such people. (What kind of reaction would you get today if you spent your time with people that our society hates?)

Lost sheep (15:4)

Jesus agreed with the Pharisees that tax collectors, prostitutes, and others had wandered away from God like sheep (Isaiah 53:6, Jeremiah 50:6). But he disagreed with the Pharisees about how to deal with them. Ezekiel 34:11-31 describes God seeking his lost sheep and caring for them, offering protection and nourishment. Though God's sheep have wandered off, he loves them and will seek them until he finds them. In fact, God says he doesn't want anyone to perish, but for all to be saved (see 2 Peter 3:9 and 1 Timothy 2:4). That was Jesus' attitude as well—is it yours?

FOR DEEPER STUDY ON YOUR OWN

1. Luke 15 contains three parables about lost things. Read the third parable found in verses 11-32. Compare and contrast its teaching with the first two parables.

---

[2]Freedman, D. N., *The Anchor Bible Dictionary.* (New York: Doubleday, 1996).

2. Read Galatians 2:11-21. Like Jesus, Peter and Paul were criticized by fellow Jews for eating with "sinners." How did Peter handle the criticism? How did Paul? How would you handle such criticism?

3. Read Jeremiah 50:6-7 and Ezekiel 34:11-31. What was God's attitude toward the lost sheep of Israel? What would it look like for you to live with that attitude toward the lost?

4. Read Matthew 9:9-13. Why did Jesus invest his limited time with immoral people? What would happen if you did that? What would your Christian friends think? How would it affect you and your family?

A WEEKLY REFLECTION

Take a minute to reflect on how well you've been doing in the following five areas of your spiritual life this week—a 10 means you did an amazing job. This reflection can serve as a spiritual gauge to help you consider some very important areas. This is for your personal evaluation and growth; it's NOT a test—no one else needs to see it.

FELLOWSHIP: CONNECTING YOUR HEART TO OTHERS'

How well did I connect with other Christians?

1   2   3   4   5   6   7   8   9   10

DISCIPLESHIP: GROWING TO BE LIKE JESUS

How well did I take steps to grow spiritually and deepen my faith on my own?

1   2   3   4   5   6   7   8   9   10

MINISTRY: SERVING OTHERS IN LOVE

How well did I recognize opportunities to serve others and follow through?

1   2   3   4   5   6   7   8   9   10

EVANGELISM: SHARING YOUR STORY AND GOD'S STORY

How well did I engage in spiritual conversations with non-Christians?

1   2   3   4   5   6   7   8   9   10

WORSHIP: SURRENDERING YOUR LIFE TO HONOR GOD

How well did I focus on God's presence and honor him with my life? Was my relationship with God a primary focus?

1   2   3   4   5   6   7   8   9   10

When you finish, celebrate the areas where you feel good and consider how you can use those strengths to help others in their journey to be more like Jesus. You might also want to take time to identify some potential areas for growth.

JESUS IN FLESH AND BLOOD

★ **LEADERS, READ PAGE 88.**

Brandon is a Christian. But based on some of his choices, you might not always think so. He comes from a divorced family and his parents both work long hours, so he doesn't have much of a relationship with either of them. He doesn't have many friends, either. Brandon chooses to express his pain by acting out at school—so he's always getting in trouble.

Out of the blue, a guy named Dylan invited Brandon to a church-based small group that met in Dylan's home. Dylan had always been nice to Brandon, so Brandon said he'd go. Dylan was excited that Brandon agreed to give it a try, and eagerly met him at the door when he arrived at the house. He introduced him to his church buddies and made him feel like he belonged.

One night after small group Brandon couldn't get a ride so Dylan volunteered to drive him home. They spent the time talking about movies and music—and Brandon carefully slipped one of Dylan's CDs into his backpack. At first,

Brandon didn't think much about the theft. But a few days later, Brandon thought about the way Dylan had been treating him—with kindness, understanding, and loyalty—and he felt guilty. Brandon wondered how he would go back and admit to Dylan that he had stolen his CD.

The following week at small group, Brandon owned up to his actions and told Dylan what he did. Without a pause Dylan said, "It's all right. Keep it, dude. I was going to give it to you anyway. I'll get another one. Thanks for telling me, though—I know that must have been tough. So, how was your week?"

Brandon was shocked. He knew this was going to be a different kind of friendship. It was only a CD, but to Brandon, Dylan's actions demonstrated the Christian love that he had heard so much about but had rarely seen in the flesh. Because of this, Brandon wanted to know Jesus even more—more like Dylan.

When God offered his love to a lost world, he came in the flesh…as Jesus. He is still present today in people like Dylan and in people like you. In this session you'll see how much God loves humanity—enough to become human himself.

♥ FELLOWSHIP: CONNECTING YOUR HEART TO OTHERS

Goal: To share about your life and listen attentively to others, caring about what they share

The Bible teaches that God came to earth in human form. His name was Jesus, and as you probably know, he arrived the way normal humans do…as a baby. God as a human is a difficult concept to imagine in today's world.

Pick one of the following questions to answer:

1. If you were God, how would you have chosen to get the world's attention? Would it have been as a baby in

a manger? Would you have arrived during the Super Bowl halftime show when the whole world was watching? Through a movie? How? Be creative in your answer.

2. Share a highlight that has happened to you since the last time the group was together.

3. Check in with your accountability partner (from last session) and see how your heart for the lost is developing.

DISCIPLESHIP: GROWING TO BE LIKE JESUS

Goal: To explore God's Word, gain biblical knowledge, and make personal applications

Have you ever heard of the *Incarnation*? Maybe not, but you've probably heard of God becoming Jesus. Well, that's the Incarnation. It's a fancy word that means "God coming as a man." Why did God come to earth as Jesus? To save the world and communicate God's love.

In the Old Testament, God communicated through the Law and through prophets (such as Isaiah and Jeremiah). But the written and spoken word was merely God's preparation for his actual *presence* among us—Jesus. He was the clearest way God could communicate his love for us.

Jesus expected his disciples to teach and do what he taught and did. He prayed for them: "My prayer is not that you take them out of the world but that you protect them from the evil one...As you sent me into the world, I have sent them into the world" (John 17:15,18). He left them on earth to *be* God's message on his behalf.

As a group, do you have any questions about the Incarnation? It's a big idea, so feel free to ask lots of questions about what it really means.

Read John 1:1-14. (If you don't have a Bible, the passage is on pages 93-94.)

1. Why do you think Jesus is called the "Word" in this passage?

2. What are some characteristics of the Word?

3. How does Jesus give light to the world? How do the verses give a specific answer to this question? What exactly is the "light"?

4. What does this passage teach us about Jesus' nature (he was and what he did)?

5. What did John the Baptist come to do (see verse 6)?

6. Read verse 10. Why did the world fail to recognize Jesus for who he was?

7. According to this passage, what does it take to become a child of God?

8. Does God speak to you? If so, how? Are you a good listener? What do you do to listen well?

9. Why is it so important that Jesus is God? Why is it important that Jesus became human?

10. How do you express your faith in Jesus? In other words, how are you a different person because of your faith?

EVANGELISM: SHARING YOUR STORY AND GOD'S STORY

Goal: To consider how the truths from this session might be applied to your relationships with unbelievers

How did Jesus spread the good news about God? "The Word became flesh and made his dwelling among us" (John 1:14). Jesus himself was the message. His life said what God wanted us to hear. He became one of us and moved into our world to show us God's true nature. We can learn a lot about our own roles as Christians in this world by studying Jesus' example.

1. In what ways are you already caring for non-Christians? Look back at the names you wrote in the evangelism section of session 1 (page 23) and add any additional names that have come to mind since the last time you were together.

What's so impor-
tant about learning
someone's story? Well,
somewhere between
that person's story and
your faith story (or testimony), there's probably
a unique intersection
that will lead to deeper
conversations about
God—God's story.

Instead of just preach-
ing *at* people, you're
caring enough about
them to learn their
stories and look for
possible connections
with your story and
God's story so they
can get to know God
as well. But in order for
that to happen, you've
got to (a) listen to their
stories, (b) know God's
story of love for human-
ity, and (c) express your
own story. All three are
equally important.

2. What can you do to go to their worlds? How can you go where they are and be part of their lives? Choose one name and give an example of how it might be done.

3. One part of becoming an evangelistic person is learning how to listen to others' stories. This requires that you actually care enough about others to learn about them. Circle two names from your list on page 23 of people whose stories you don't yet know. Share those names with your accountability partner and make it a goal to ask them to share their life stories with you before the next time you meet.

MINISTRY: SERVING OTHERS IN LOVE

Goal: To recognize and take advantage of opportunities to serve others

Below is a list of actions that might identify someone as a Christian. You might say these are habits of a follower of Christ. Choose one that you currently struggle with. After you share that one habit with the group, try to practice it this week. As you practice it, consider writing down your feelings about it on one of the journal pages in the back of this book.

- Greet people who are not your friends. How easily do kind greetings and smiles come to your lips?
- If you regularly encounter someone you don't know, ask his or her name. Write it down so you can greet this person by name next time.
- When you are in the wrong, apologize.
- When someone offends you, offer mercy instead of judgment.
- Be generous, especially to those who don't deserve it.
- When you say you'll do something, do it.
- Tell the truth, even when it would be to your advantage to lie.
- Go out of your way to be kind to someone you don't like, or better yet, who doesn't like you.
- Take time to listen to someone.
- Serve others by doing things like helping them with schoolwork, holding doors open for them, asking how you can help, and so on.

☖ WORSHIP: SURRENDERING YOUR LIFE TO HONOR GOD

Goal: To focus on God's presence

God becoming flesh in the person of Jesus is an important truth. It's a huge thing that God loves you so much that *he became like you to reach you* (except he is perfect, and we're not). That truth alone is worthy of your praise!

1. John 1:14 is a verse that you'll want to know when referring to God becoming human (the Incarnation, remember?). *The Message* paraphrase is very different from what you read in the New International Version. Read *The Message* paraphrase below (of John 1:14) and then share what you like or don't like about it. Does it clear things up or make it more confusing?

> THE WORD BECAME FLESH AND BLOOD,
> AND MOVED INTO THE NEIGHBORHOOD.
> WE SAW THE GLORY WITH OUR OWN EYES,
> THE ONE-OF-A-KIND GLORY,
> LIKE FATHER, LIKE SON,
> GENEROUS INSIDE AND OUT,
> TRUE FROM START TO FINISH.

2. If you have time, write John 1:14 in your own words.

3. Close your time in prayer—and be sure to thank God for his amazing love expressed in Jesus.

AT HOME THIS WEEK

Option 1: A Weekly Reflection

Take another self-evaluation that reflects five areas of your spiritual life (fellowship, discipleship, ministry, evangelism, and worship). See pages 43-44.

Option 2: Daily Bible Readings

Check out the Bible reading plan on pages 114-115.

Option 3: Memory Verses

Memorize another verse from pages 119-120.

Option 4: Journaling

Choose one or more of the following options:

- Write down whatever is on your mind.

- Read your journal entry from last week and write a reflection about it.
- Respond to these questions: What is your own personal definition of *Incarnation*? When I see what God went through to reach me, it makes me want to...

Option 5: Wrap It Up

Write out your answers to any questions that you didn't answer during your small group time.

LEARN A LITTLE MORE

The Word (John 1:1)

Understanding this title for Jesus could take a lifetime of study! Let's start with this: Just as no person has ever seen God (John 1:18), no person can know another person's thoughts. However, our words reveal our invisible thoughts to others. Therefore, Jesus is called the Word—because he makes the invisible (that is, God) visible.

The Bible also says that the Word existed before the creation of the world—and not only that, the Word was involved with the creative work itself. (In Genesis' creation account, notice that everything was created by God *speaking*—again, words.) Colossians 1:16, in reference to Jesus, reads: "For by him all things were created: things in heaven and on earth, visible and invisible, whether thrones or powers or rulers or authorities; all things were created by him and for him."

Darkness has not understood it (1:5)

Darkness is a common biblical description for those who live without God. It's no wonder that people who have grown up in darkness have trouble understanding us if we simply start talking to them about Jesus. It takes much more than our words to convince people who are used to darkness that it's worth giving up for what we have in God—which is light.

John (1:6)

The John referenced in this passage is not John, the author of this Gospel (who was one of the disciples), but rather John the Baptist—one of the most important characters in biblical history:

- All four Gospel accounts associate John with the beginning of the gospel.
- Jesus claimed that John was more than a prophet and, from a human point of view, the greatest human being ever.
- Unlike other major New Testament characters, the deaths of Jesus and John are given significant treatment.
- John was Jesus' first cousin; his mother was Mary's sister, Elizabeth.
- John still had followers after his death.

His own (1:11)

His own refers to the Jewish people.

Children of God (1:12)

Some people teach that all human beings are children of God. Though it's true that God created all of us in his image and for his purposes, Ephesians 2:3-5 says human beings are by nature children of wrath (which means spiritually dead because of our sin). Only through faith in Jesus are we reunited with God and adopted as his children (Galatians 3:26-4:7, Ephesians 1:5). Therefore we are born as *creations* of God, but when we put our faith in Jesus we are adopted as *children* of God.

FOR DEEPER STUDY ON YOUR OWN

1. Read Genesis 1:1. What are the similarities between Genesis 1:1 and John 1:1?

2. Check out the following passages to see the power of God's word: Psalm 33:6, Psalm 119:89, Isaiah 40:8, and Hebrews 4:12-13.

A WEEKLY REFLECTION

Take a minute to reflect on how well you've been doing in the following five areas of your spiritual life this week—a 10 means you did an amazing job. This reflection can serve as a spiritual gauge to help you consider some very important areas. This is for your personal evaluation and growth; it's NOT a test—no one else needs to see it.

FELLOWSHIP: CONNECTING YOUR HEART TO OTHERS

How well did I connect with other Christians?

1   2   3   4   5   6   7   8   9   10

DISCIPLESHIP: GROWING TO BE LIKE JESUS

How well did I take steps to grow spiritually and deepen my faith on my own?

1   2   3   4   5   6   7   8   9   10

MINISTRY: SERVING OTHERS IN LOVE

How well did I recognize opportunities to serve others and follow through?

1   2   3   4   5   6   7   8   9   10

EVANGELISM: SHARING YOUR STORY AND GOD'S STORY

How well did I engage in spiritual conversations with non-Christians?

1   2   3   4   5   6   7   8   9   10

WORSHIP: SURRENDERING YOUR LIFE TO HONOR GOD

How well did I focus on God's presence and honor him with my life? Was my relationship with God a primary focus?

1   2   3   4   5   6   7   8   9   10

When you finish, celebrate the areas where you feel good and consider how you can use those strengths to help others in their journey to be more like Jesus. You might also want to take time to identify some potential areas for growth.

SOWING SEEDS

⭐ **LEADERS, READ PAGE 88.**

Amy and Brandy have been best friends since the sixth grade. Amy's family has gone to church for as long as she can remember. But Amy has never really taken her faith seriously and made it her own. Most often she went to church because her parents made her. Brandy, on the other hand, has never been to church and her parents are not Christians. In the five years that Amy and Brandy had been friends, God, faith, and religion were never discussed.

Then, at the end of last summer, things changed.

Amy came home from youth camp where she dealt seriously with her faith for the first time. She returned with a new outlook on her relationship with God—she wanted to be closer to him, learn more about Jesus, and allow her new faith to influence the way she lived her life. She was very excited—and at the same time, a little bit nervous to share her faith with Brandy. Amy enthusiastically overloaded Brandy with every detail of camp life. And she told Brandy about her new commitment and how she wanted to live a life that was honoring to God.

Brandy was happy for her friend but didn't really understand all that had happened at camp. Feeling uncomfortable, Brandy began to back away from Amy and their friendship. So Amy decided to be open and honest about her faith while being sensitive to Brandy's questions and confusion.

Amy was amazed at how their new discussions regarding spiritual matters flowed so naturally. Amy realized she didn't need to overwhelm Brandy with everything at once and instead viewed their times together as slowly planting seeds and watering them with more love and conversation—all in God's timing.

Many people teach that evangelism happens by sharing a few facts about God and using Bible verses to try to convince non-Christians to pray a prayer that assures entrance into heaven. Actually, evangelism is a lot bigger than that—and more mysterious...because God is involved.

One way to bring people closer to Jesus is to look for opportunities to plant seeds about God and then allow God's Spirit to provide the water needed to help the seeds develop—just like Amy began doing with Brandy. And that's what this session is all about...taking time to plant seeds.

FELLOWSHIP: CONNECTING YOUR HEART TO OTHERS

Goal: To share about your life and listen attentively to others, caring about what they share

The passage you're about to study contains a farming illustration by Jesus. So to get you thinking about farming, share one of the following three options that best fits your current mood (or your memory). Be wise with your time and talk about just one of the following.

1. Share any story that has you driving a tractor. Most boys grow up dreaming of being able to operate large equipment. Do you have a story? If so, share it briefly.

2. Share any farm experience you've had—milking cows, being chased by a pig, sleeping in a barn, or something along those lines.

3. Let's say you lived on a farm that could only grow one crop—what would it be? Why?

DISCIPLESHIP: GROWING TO BE LIKE JESUS

Goal: To explore God's Word, gain biblical knowledge, and make personal applications

Jesus' original audience was full of farmers and fishermen, so it's not surprising that he told stories about farm life and fishing to illustrate his central points. He was a genius at discussing spiritual realities in familiar, nonreligious language that was easy to remember. (Many of these illustrations came in the form of parables—see page 53.)

Read Matthew 13:1-23. (If you don't have a Bible, the passage is on pages 94-95.)

1. Why do you think Jesus taught with parables? What are some benefits of teaching with stories? How does this text support your answer?

2. What do you think Jesus meant in verse 9 when he said, "He who has ears, let him hear"?

3. Based on verses 11-12, why did Jesus teach to the crowds? Why didn't he just teach the disciples?

4. In verse 11, Jesus talked about "you" and "them"—that

is, the disciples and the crowds. Based on the words quoted from Isaiah in verse 15, what is the difference between the crowds and the disciples?

5. What does the soil represent in this parable?

6. Of the four soils mentioned in this parable, which one best describes your heart right now? How receptive are you to spiritual things?

7. Think for a moment about the seed thrown along the rocky places—growth without roots. What does it mean to "grow roots" after hearing God's Word? What are some clues from the text that will help you answer this question?

8. In your own words, what is the "message about the kingdom" (verse 18)?

9. Based on this parable, what is your responsibility when you listen to a message or sermon?

10. It seems that persecution can either build up or tear down one's faith. What makes the difference? Can you share an example from your own life?

EVANGELISM: SHARING YOUR STORY AND GOD'S STORY

Goal: To consider how the truths from this session might be applied to your relationships with unbelievers

Jesus rarely explained his entire message at once. He understood that his listeners would be overwhelmed. Instead he planted seeds—small pieces of his message—and gave the seeds time to sprout. If we think of faith in Jesus as a large tree that grows in a person's life over time, we can imagine everything we say to non-Christians about God as sowing seeds.

One of the most important ways we can sow seeds of the gospel in others' lives is to discuss common human experiences. These subjects naturally lead to spiritual conversations that are neither preachy nor religious. These conversations may not even contain the whole gospel message at one time. They are simply seeds—and it's God's job to make them grow. Our only job is to plant them.

1. Try something kind of risky: Role-play. Take two people in the group and have a conversation as the group listens in. One person is the Christian and the other person is the non-Christian friend. You can begin with a typical question like, "How was your day?" While the non-Christian answers, look for opportunities to plant small spiritual seeds. Try this for about two minutes and then discuss what happened. It might feel awkward, it could be funny, but the purpose is to help you look for ways within a conversation to plant spiritual seeds. Give each other feedback and plenty of encouragement. This is a hard skill to learn!

2. How does planting seeds fit with what you talked about in session 2 on page 37? Remember the three stories?
    a. Listening to your friend's story
    b. Sharing your story
    c. Shedding light on God's story
    During the sharing of these three stories, there will most likely be a time when the stories intersect and point to God. How might this idea work with the principle of planting seeds?

3. Talking about spiritual things in ordinary language is a skill you can learn with practice. For example, how would you respond if one of your non-Christian friends said to you tomorrow at school, "What did you do last night?" Which of the following is planting a seed?

a. "Not much. A little homework and then I went out."
b. "I went to a Bible study. We studied how Jesus spread the gospel, and we prayed for our non-Christian friends...like you."
c. "I have this group of friends who meet weekly to talk about God and how we can live life with more meaning and purpose. It's great to have friends who really care about my life...even my spiritual life."

If you chose (a)...You are probably not planting seeds at all, right? (Wrong! You did plant something.)

If you chose (b)...This is an honest answer, but a non-Christian probably doesn't know what the word *gospel* means. Also, it makes you sound like you're religious and trying to "get" the person.

If you chose (c)...This answer is also honest and will probably provoke much more curiosity. Who doesn't want a group of friends who care about your life? Everybody does! You just planted a seed.

MINISTRY: SERVING OTHERS IN LOVE

Goal: To recognize and take advantage of opportunities to serve others

Imagine that you talk about spiritual things with 20 friends. Ten of them have hearts as hard as the path; they're not interested in anything spiritual. Five of them are like rocky soil; they go to church with you for a while and say they love it, but when God doesn't make their lives easy, they decide he's not worth their time. Four friends become consistent churchgoers, but they chase "the good life" and love to party and drink on the weekends. Only one out of those 20 friends becomes a faithful follower of Jesus.

1. How would you handle that? Would you:

   - Feel rejected?
   - Feel hurt?
   - Get frustrated?
   - Blame yourself?
   - Feel good about your faithfulness, regardless of the outcome?
   - Give up?
   - Persevere?
   - Other:

2. How can you encourage others in your group when they experience this type of rejection? How do group members care for each other when they're trying to follow Jesus' example and the results are bad?

WORSHIP: SURRENDERING YOUR LIFE TO HONOR GOD

Goal: To focus on God's presence

Jesus teaches us how to pray for non-Christians. For example, the story of the four soils suggests what we can ask God to do in the hearts of different people:

   a. soften hard soil,
   b. break up rocks that keep the seed from sinking deeply in,
   c. tear out thorns, and
   d. help sincere seekers get past obstacles and the temptation of following after "the good life."

1. In a conversation with a non-Christian, listening is probably even more important than talking. You can practice your listening skills here in this group right now. Allow everyone to answer this question: "How can we pray for you this week?" As people share, practice listening closely rather than thinking about what you'd like to say next.

2. Pray for the shared requests. Ask God to give you wisdom to know when to plant seeds with the friends you listed in session 1.

AT HOME THIS WEEK

Option 1: A Weekly Reflection

Take another self-evaluation that reflects five areas of your spiritual life (fellowship, discipleship, ministry, evangelism, and worship). See pages 55-56.

Option 2: Daily Bible Readings

Check out the Bible reading plan on pages 114-115.

Option 3: Memory Verses

Memorize another verse from pages 119-120.

Option 4: Journaling

Choose one or more of the following options:

- Write down whatever is on your mind.
- Read your journal entry from last week and write a reflection about it.
- Finish these statements: I typically miss opportunities to plant seeds because... The soil that best represents my spiritual life right now is...

Option 5: Wrap It Up

Write out your answers to any questions that you didn't answer during your small group time.

LEARN A LITTLE MORE

Parables (Matthew 13:3)

The word *parable* comes from two Greek words meaning "to throw alongside." Parables are simple word pictures, stories, or illustrations thrown alongside a spiritual truth. Parables make both the truth and the picture difficult to forget. As one of Jesus' favorite teaching methods, parables forced people to move from passive listening to active thinking. When reading a parable (and you'll come across more than 40 in the Gospels) it is important to avoid two pitfalls: (1) ignoring important details, and (2) trying to make every detail mean something.

Sow (13:3)

In ancient Israel, farmers sowed their seed by hand. They tossed the seed freely to the ground, knowing that not all of it would fall on good soil. They tilled (tore up) the soil afterward to make the seeds sink into the dirt. Today's farmers till first and then carefully sow seed in the soil, but that wasn't the method in Jesus' day. To us, scattering seed on hard ground seems wasteful—and talking about spiritual things with hardhearted people may seem wasteful, too. (It's not!)

Seed (13:3)

The gospel—the message about God's kingdom and how to enter it—is the seed. When received, it brings salvation.

Scattered seed (13:4)

Most of us don't identify with a culture centered on farming; therefore this parable may be confusing at first. But in ancient Israel, during the non-growing season, people would walk on the land instead of going around the growth area. This created paths in the middle of the farm. Then when it was time for the farmer to plant his seed, he would walk around with a bag of seed and scatter it everywhere, even off the edges of the good land, in hopes of gaining more crops. In the minds of Jesus' original listeners, this parable was understandable because he used an example that came from their everyday lives.

Soil (13:5)

People respond differently to the gospel. Depending on the condition of their hearts, they may reject it, receive it superficially, or fully embrace it and let it change their lives. The soil represents someone's life and heart.

Kingdom of heaven (13:11)

The kingdom of heaven is everything under God's rule and possessing his presence. Most of Jesus' teaching centered upon explaining the nature of the kingdom. The kingdom arrived on earth with Jesus (Matthew 4:17) and exists within every believer (Matthew 12:28). The kingdom is spiritual, not physical—you won't find it on a map, and it can't be put on one.

FOR DEEPER STUDY ON YOUR OWN

1. Check out other parables that talk about the kingdom of God:

   - Matthew 13:24-35,44-52
   - Matthew 18:23-35
   - Matthew 20:1-16
   - Matthew 22:2-14
   - Luke 13:18-30

2. Read Isaiah 6:8-13, in which God gives the prophet his life assignment. Why do you suppose God gives him instructions to proclaim the truth to people God knew wouldn't listen? What does this passage have to do with Matthew 13?

3. Ezekiel 2:3-7 describes the prophet Ezekiel's assignment. How is it like Isaiah's? How is it like Jesus'? How is it like yours?

A WEEKLY REFLECTION

Take a minute to reflect on how well you've been doing in the following five areas of your spiritual life this week—a 10 means you did an amazing job. This reflection can serve as a spiritual gauge to help you consider some very important areas. This is for your personal evaluation and growth; it's NOT a test—no one else needs to see it.

FELLOWSHIP: CONNECTING YOUR HEART TO OTHERS'

How well did I connect with other Christians?

1   2   3   4   5   6   7   8   9   10

DISCIPLESHIP: GROWING TO BE LIKE JESUS

How well did I take steps to grow spiritually and deepen my faith on my own?

1   2   3   4   5   6   7   8   9   10

MINISTRY: SERVING OTHERS IN LOVE

How well did I recognize opportunities to serve others and follow through?

1   2   3   4   5   6   7   8   9   10

EVANGELISM: SHARING YOUR STORY AND GOD'S STORY

How well did I engage in spiritual conversations with non-Christians?

1   2   3   4   5   6   7   8   9   10

WORSHIP: SURRENDERING YOUR LIFE TO HONOR GOD

How well did I focus on God's presence and honor him with my life? Was my relationship with God a primary focus?

1   2   3   4   5   6   7   8   9   10

When you finish, celebrate the areas where you feel good and consider how you can use those strengths to help others in their journey to be more like Jesus. You might also want to take time to identify some potential areas for growth.

WHO IS MY NEIGHBOR?

⭐ **LEADERS, READ PAGE 88.**

Katie lived in a culturally diverse neighborhood. A few families were from Egypt, one was from Japan, another neighbor was Chinese, and others were from somewhere outside the country—but she didn't know where just yet. Katie didn't interact much with her neighbors because she was intensely shy. She went to school with some of their children, but she didn't even know what to say to them. When her youth group announced "bring your neighbor to church" month, Katie panicked.

What if they already have their own beliefs? she thought. What if they're offended by me asking what they believe or if they want to go to church with me? Maybe they don't like me because I'm an American and a Christian. Katie had many questions about how her neighbors might respond.

One weekend her neighborhood had a large community garage sale. As she walked to some of the houses to see what they were selling, she noticed how interesting some of the items were from the families of different cultures. She decided to be brave and asked about their heritages and family customs. She met a girl her own age named Samira whose family was from Egypt. They hit it if off and made plans to walk to school together.

As Katie got to know Samira better, she realized they were more alike than different. This neighborhood friendship gave Katie confidence and helped lessen her shyness and fear. Plus, Katie didn't get rejected when she asked Samira to church. Samira had a great time and has a lot of questions about God.

This session is about looking for opportunities to share Jesus with people who are different from you. Regardless of your skin color, nationality, or background, your challenge is to get to know people who not only look different from you, but also come from different parts of the world. Unfortunately there isn't much diversity in American churches. And yet the body of Christ as a whole is diverse—and it's worldwide.

Be a part of it.

FELLOWSHIP: CONNECTING YOUR HEART TO OTHERS

Goal: To share about your life and listen attentively to others, caring about what they share

It's a sad reality in today's world that racism still exists—often blatantly so. It should be obvious to Christians that there's no place for racist attitudes in their lives. One of Jesus' commands is to love each other as he loves us. While it's often difficult to love like that, it's a worthy (and necessary) pursuit for a follower of Christ.

1. Can you discuss a positive interaction you've had with someone from a different ethnic group? Take one minute to share part of the story with the group.

2. How does racism make you feel?

DISCIPLESHIP: GROWING TO BE LIKE JESUS

Goal: To explore God's Word, gain biblical knowledge, and make personal applications

It's normal to prefer to spend time with people who are like us—after all, it's comfortable! It's also natural to create "us versus them" ways of thinking without meaning to. We do this to protect our comfort zones, but this exclusion can blind us to others' needs. In this session's passage, we'll see the tragedy of indifference. Jesus calls us to love everyone, regardless of whether they're "like us."

Read Luke 10:25-37. (If you don't have a Bible, the passage is on page 95-96.)

1. What's your first impression of this parable? What kinds of things stand out to you?

2. Why do you think this person was testing Jesus with these questions?

3. How is the teaching of the parable ("Who is my neighbor?") connected with the introduction ("What must I do to inherit eternal life?")?

4. Why do you think the priest and the Levite passed by the wounded man?

5. Why do you think the Samaritan stopped? What might have motivated him?

6. Why did Jesus use a Samaritan character in this parable? What is the significance of that choice? (Skip ahead and read the study note on Samaritans under "Learn a Little More" to help answer these questions.)

7. How does this parable answer the neighbor question? Based on this text, how would you answer the teacher of the law in your own words?

8. What do you think this passage tells us about following God's ways?

9. What does it tell us about love?

10. Who are some people you would not consider neighbors? Explain your answer.

11. This is a tough question, but be honest: Do you ever find yourself making excuses for not liking others who aren't like you? Explain.

EVANGELISM: SHARING YOUR STORY AND GOD'S STORY

Goal: To consider how the truths from this session might be applied to your relationships with unbelievers

Jesus said all of life is summed up in how we love God and our neighbors. The traditional Jewish interpretation of "neighbor" was a fellow Jew, but Jesus' story illustrates why that interpretation of neighbor is too narrow.

1. Where do you currently see racist attitudes within your (a) campus, (b) church, and (c) community?

2. How do you see ethnic diversity at your school?

3. As a group, talk about ways that you might cross ethnic barriers (if they exist) within your church. If your church currently has strong diversity (many ethnic groups interacting and participating), make sure you praise God for a great picture of the body of Christ. If it's happening in your church, it's a rare church—and a great one!

MINISTRY: SERVING OTHERS IN LOVE

Goal: To recognize and take advantage of opportunities to serve others

Choose one of the following ideas to carry out as a group, or follow through with one of the ideas on your own.

- Have a dinner or party and invite people of different colors, cultures, or backgrounds.
- If you have a college campus nearby, contact the office that handles international students and find out how you can help those students feel welcome in your country.
- Walk through a neighborhood ethnically different from your own and pray for the people who live there—as well as for your understanding and acceptance of those who aren't like you.
- Choose a missionary and write to her, encouraging her pursuits to love others who live in a different culture.
- Consider financially supporting a missionary as a group.
- Other:

WORSHIP: SURRENDERING YOUR LIFE TO HONOR GOD

Goal: To focus on God's presence

1. Which of the following two prayers do you need to pray more often?

"GOD, HELP ME TO LOVE THOSE WHO ARE NOT LIKE ME."

"GOD, PLEASE HELP ME TO BE BRAVE ENOUGH TO TELL OTHERS ABOUT YOU (WHETHER THEY'RE LIKE ME OR NOT)."

2. Share your answer with the group and then pray for each other before you leave.

AT HOME THIS WEEK

Option 1: A Weekly Reflection

Take another self-evaluation that reflects five areas of your spiritual life (fellowship, discipleship, ministry, evangelism, and worship). See pages 65-66.

Option 2: Daily Bible Readings

Check out the Bible reading plan on pages 114-115.

Option 3: Memory Verses

Memorize another verse from pages 119-120.

Option 4: Journaling

Choose one or more of the following options:

- Write down whatever is on your mind.
- Read your journal entry from last week and write a reflection about it.
- Complete these sentences: I occasionally find myself being prejudiced when I... God, please help me to...

Option 5: Wrap It Up

Write out your answers to any questions that you didn't answer during your small group time.

LEARN A LITTLE MORE

The Law (Luke 10:26)

"The Law" refers to the Law of Moses, which contains exactly 613 laws. Most people are familiar with the Ten Commandments, which served as an introduction or overview of the Law. For the Jewish nation, the Law wasn't simply a set of religious rules—the Law defined their culture.

The single purpose of the Law was to define the terms of the relationship between God and his people. The Law also exposed the difference between sin and perfection. If you wanted a relationship with God, you had to be perfect since God is perfect. You'd have to follow *all of the law, all of the time.*

You're probably thinking, *No one is perfect, so what good is the Law?* You're right! The Law can't save anyone; it can only show us how imperfect we are. Without ever seeing the light, it's impossible to know you're in the dark.

Jesus came to us and lived a perfect life; he never broke a single command, whether by his actions or thoughts. When we have faith in Jesus, his death pays the price for our imperfections (sin). Then when God looks at us, he only sees the perfection of Jesus. In the end, the Law is upheld—but not by us.

From Jerusalem to Jericho (10:30)

This was a notoriously dangerous road. It passed through desert country, steep gorges, and sharp rocks. One slip could cost you your life. Also, it was a likely place for a robbery. Nobody was around to help—you were totally on your own.

Priest...Levite (10:31-32)

The priest and Levite were Jews who worked at the temple and strictly followed Jewish law. If they touched corpses, non-Jews, or anyone else unclean by the Law's standards, they wouldn't be able to do their jobs until they went through a ritual cleansing—and that cleansing would cost them both money and effort. However, Jewish tradition highly valued hospitality to strangers, and most rabbis would have taught that kindness in this case was more important than being momentarily unclean.

Samaritan (10:33)

After the death of King Solomon in 933 B.C., Israel divided into two countries. The northern kingdom retained the name Israel, and the southern kingdom was called Judah. The capital of the northern kingdom was Samaria, which was defeated by the Assyrians in 722. When one nation defeated another, the common practice was to deport (get rid of) as many leaders and influential people as possible so an uprising wouldn't occur. Over the course of 700 years, the Jews who were not deported intermarried with the Assyrians and Canaanites (people who lived in Israel before the Israelites arrived). This new mix of people (part Jew, part Assyrian) were called Samantans. The Jews despised the Samaritans and avoided them at all costs. They saw Samaritans as half-breeds who had given up their Jewish heritage and "purity." Jesus' parable was highly offensive to his original listeners because it called into question their hatred of the Samaritans—a group very different from themselves.

FOR DEEPER STUDY ON YOUR OWN

1. Read the original context of "love your neighbor" in Leviticus 19:13-18. How many ways does this text show us how to love our neighbors? List them. How different would it be to live in a society in which you were expected to only treat your own ethnic group like this?

2. Read Proverbs 14:21. If you despise a neighbor, how could you deal with that person differently?

3. How would you answer the questions Jesus asks in Matthew 5:46-47? Why do you think he makes such a big deal about this?

4. What motivation for reaching out to ethnically different people do you find in 2 Corinthians 5:14-21? What about in James 2:8-11?

A WEEKLY REFLECTION

Take a minute to reflect on how well you've been doing in the following five areas of your spiritual life this week—a 10 means you did an amazing job. This reflection can serve as a spiritual gauge to help you consider some very important areas. This is for your personal evaluation and growth; it's NOT a test—no one else needs to see it.

FELLOWSHIP: CONNECTING YOUR HEART TO OTHERS'

How well did I connect with other Christians?

1   2   3   4   5   6   7   8   9   10

DISCIPLESHIP: GROWING TO BE LIKE JESUS

How well did I take steps to grow spiritually and deepen my faith on my own?

1   2   3   4   5   6   7   8   9   10

MINISTRY: SERVING OTHERS IN LOVE

How well did I recognize opportunities to serve others and follow through?

1　2　3　4　5　6　7　8　9　10

EVANGELISM: SHARING YOUR STORY AND GOD'S STORY

How well did I engage in spiritual conversations with non-Christians?

1　2　3　4　5　6　7　8　9　10

WORSHIP: SURRENDERING YOUR LIFE TO HONOR GOD

How well did I focus on God's presence and honor him with my life? Was my relationship with God a primary focus?

1　2　3　4　5　6　7　8　9　10

When you finish, celebrate the areas where you feel good and consider how you can use those strengths to help others in their journey to be more like Jesus. You might also want to take time to identify some potential areas for growth.

TEAMING UP

⭐ **LEADERS, READ PAGE 88.**

During their junior year of high school, Taylor and Erik played on the football team. They quickly became good friends because of this common bond they shared. They often talked about their faith and desire to share the good news of God's love with others. They both thought it was helpful to have a friend who shared similar goals; they needed the encouragement because many days they felt beaten down by their peers and were unsure if they were making a difference in spreading God's love.

One Friday night they decided to invite some of the guys from the team over to Erik's house to play pool, cards, and video games. Erik and Taylor wanted to get to know the guys better and look for opportunities to listen to their stories, as well as to share their own faith stories and eventually point out God's love story. Together, Taylor and Erik were strong enough to withstand some of their teammates' questions—and joking. Because it was a great success, Erik and Taylor began hosting this get-together every Friday night. They slowly gained their teammates' respect, and a few of them came to know Jesus as Savior.

God never asks us to face the world on our own. In this session you'll consider how Jesus' practice of sending his disciples out in teams serves as a good example for you and another Christ-following friend.

♥ FELLOWSHIP: CONNECTING YOUR HEART TO OTHERS

Goal: To share about your life and listen attentively to others, caring about what they share

By this point, you've either been challenged to have spiritual conversations with non-Christians, or you've been turned off and/or scared by this whole idea of evangelism.

Choose one of the following options and share your answer with the group:

1. Share what you've been learning as a result of this group going through this book.

2. Share about a spiritual conversation you've had with a non-Christian since beginning to work through the material in this book.

3. Share your fears, frustrations, or even lack of interest regarding evangelism.

DISCIPLESHIP: GROWING TO BE LIKE JESUS

Goal: To explore God's Word, gain biblical knowledge, and make personal applications

Many of us find it scary to launch into a spiritual conversation all by ourselves. We're so afraid of blowing it and saying the wrong thing that our minds go completely blank. But Jesus never intended his disciples to be solo evangelists. He expected them to make it a team effort. In fact, he said non-Christians would find their message far more convincing if they could see how the disciples interacted with each other and loved one another (John 13:34-35, 17:22-23). It's not surprising, then, that Jesus sent them out to preach in pairs.

Read Luke 10:1-12. (If you don't have a Bible, the passage is on page 96.)

1. Why do you think Jesus sent out his disciples in pairs?

2. Jesus didn't allow them to take supplies—such as money or shoes. Why do you think he gave them this rule?

3. Does this passage mean we should never plan our trips or take along supplies? Should we always just trust that God will provide?

4. What's the difference between faith (trusting God to provide) and responsibility (doing our part to be prepared)? When should you act in faith (like the 72 in this passage) and when should you act with good planning?

5. In what ways is it easier to have a partner to help you in your spiritual journey?

6. When you read in verse 2, "the workers are few," what is your response? What is a faithful worker? Do you feel like you are a faithful worker? Explain why you feel the way you do.

7. In verse 3, Jesus sent out the 72 saying they were like "lambs among wolves." What kind of barriers have you run into on your campus when it comes to living a Christian lifestyle?

8. In your opinion, what makes a good ministry partner? What qualities would your ideal partner possess?

9. What are some practical things ministry partners can do to strengthen and support each other?

10. Do you have a ministry partner? Who is it, and how well are you supporting each other?

EVANGELISM: SHARING YOUR STORY AND GOD'S STORY

Goal: To consider how the truths from this session might be applied to your relationships with unbelievers

It's likely that you aren't ready to go on the road without luggage, as Jesus' first disciples did. But there are things you *can* do in pairs that will contribute to the spread of the gospel in ways you could never foresee.

1. Spend some time talking about what you might be able to do together (evangelistically) that would be easier than doing alone. Write your ideas here.

2. Take a minute to comment on the accountability partner idea introduced in session 1. Have you two been meeting? Has it been working? Why, or why not?

3. See if anyone is up for this idea: When you finish session 6 of this study, why not take a six-week break from your own small group to lead a new group? Pair up, and tell your current leader that you're willing to lead a new group of students through the first book in this series, *Beginning in Jesus*. It's a good guide for those with spiritual questions (e.g., some of your non-Christian friends), and it's suitable for Christians as well.

MINISTRY: SERVING OTHERS IN LOVE

Goal: To recognize and take advantage of opportunities to serve others

In the Scripture passage that you studied, there's no mention of the many people who must have opened up their homes and provided food to the disciples who traveled to spread the gospel. It almost assumed that there would be people within the church who would open their hearts, homes, and wallets to help those who were doing the work of evangelism. Other New Testament books describe Christians with the spiritual gift of hospitality who gladly open their homes for those spreading the gospel. The disciples who went out in pairs depended greatly on fellow believers with that specific spiritual gift.

1. Do you know anyone in your church with the spiritual gift of hospitality? If so, who? Is there anything your group can do to encourage him in his efforts to continue to care for and support people who do God's work?

2. Is there anything you can do personally to encourage those who have specific callings to evangelistic lifestyles? How can you encourage them and/or minister to them, even if you don't have the gift of hospitality?

🚶 WORSHIP: SURRENDERING YOUR LIFE TO HONOR GOD

Goal: To focus on God's presence

1. How can the group pray for you this week?

2. Remember to pray for the non-Christians in your lives. (You might want to go back to the worship section of session 1 and see if there have been any answers to prayers that you can celebrate.)

3. Pray for those who might take the challenge and lead a new group through *Beginning in Jesus*.

AT HOME THIS WEEK

Option 1: A Weekly Reflection

Take another self-evaluation that reflects five areas of your spiritual life (fellowship, discipleship, ministry, evangelism, and worship). See pages 74-75.

Option 2: Daily Bible Readings

Check out the Bible reading plan on pages 114-115.

Option 3: Memory Verses

Memorize another verse from pages 119-120.

Option 4: Journaling

Choose one or more of the following options:

- Write down whatever is on your mind.
- Read your journal entry from last week and write a reflection about it.
- Complete these statements: My biggest fear of evangelism on my own is… If I could choose anyone in the world to partner with me, it would be…because…

Option 5: Wrap It Up

Write out your answers to any questions that you didn't answer during your small group time.

LEARN A LITTLE MORE

The seventy two (Luke 10:1)
Luke's is the only Gospel that mentions the ministry of a larger group of Jesus followers.

Do not greet anyone along the road (10:4)

"Greeting no one on the way indicates the urgency of their mission representing God and not themselves; it was offensive to withhold greetings, and pious people tried to be the first to greet an approaching person. (Jewish teachers agreed, however, that one should not interrupt religious duties like prayer in order to greet someone.)"[3]

Sodom (10:12)

During the days of Abraham, the people of Sodom (and Gomorrah) were known for their wickedness: "So the LORD told Abraham, 'I have heard a great outcry from Sodom and Gomorrah, because their sin is so flagrant'" (Genesis 18:20, NLT). God's plan was to destroy both cities for their disobedience. But Abraham asked God if he would reconsider if there were just 10 righteous people there, and God agreed. Because there were not even 10—in fact, not even one—God destroyed both cities. (See Genesis 18:16-19:29 for the whole story.)

Lambs among wolves (10:3)

Jesus' disciples were innocent and vulnerable, especially in the world. Some people, acting on Satan's behalf, would treat them harshly because of their message of Good News. The world is enemy territory.

Jesus said, "If the world hates you, keep in mind that it hated me first. If you belonged to the world, it would love you as its own. As it is, you do not belong to the world, but I have chosen you out of the world. That is why the world hates you" (John 15:18-19). We are still left in the world to reach out and make disciples of all people, in spite of the dangers. Our hope is secure, as "the one who is in you is greater than the one who is in the world" (1 John 4:4).

[3]Keener, C. S., & InterVarsity Press. *The IVP Bible Background Commentary: New Testament* (Luke 10:4). (Downers Grove, Ill.: InterVarsity Press, 1993).

FOR DEEPER STUDY ON YOUR OWN

1. Read about the Lord's judgment on Sodom in Genesis 18:16-19:29.

2. Read Matthew 10:5-31. What instructions from Jesus does Matthew add that you didn't study in the Luke passage? Clearly, spreading Jesus' message was dangerous in those days. What risks do you face today? What reasons does Jesus give for not being afraid?

3. Read John 13:34-35 and 17:22-23. What did Jesus add here about the potential of working in teams to communicate the gospel that individuals can't accomplish on their own?

A WEEKLY REFLECTION

Take a minute to reflect on how well you've been doing in the following five areas of your spiritual life this week—a 10 means you did an amazing job. This reflection can serve as a spiritual gauge to help you consider some very important areas. This is for your personal evaluation and growth; it's NOT a test—no one else needs to see it.

FELLOWSHIP: CONNECTING YOUR HEART TO OTHERS

How well did I connect with other Christians?

1   2   3   4   5   6   7   8   9   10

DISCIPLESHIP: GROWING TO BE LIKE JESUS

How well did I take steps to grow spiritually and deepen my faith on my own?

1   2   3   4   5   6   7   8   9   10

MINISTRY: SERVING OTHERS IN LOVE

How well did I recognize opportunities to serve others and follow through?

1   2   3   4   5   6   7   8   9   10

EVANGELISM: SHARING YOUR STORY AND GOD'S STORY

How well did I engage in spiritual conversations with non-Christians?

1   2   3   4   5   6   7   8   9   10

WORSHIP: SURRENDERING YOUR LIFE TO HONOR GOD

How well did I focus on God's presence and honor him with my life? Was my relationship with God a primary focus?

1   2   3   4   5   6   7   8   9   10

When you finish, celebrate the areas where you feel good and consider how you can use those strengths to help others in their journey to be more like Jesus. You might also want to take time to identify some potential areas for growth.

SESSION 6

UP A TREE

 LEADERS, READ PAGE 88.

Jobee has been a Christian since she was a child and has always taken her commitment to God seriously. She loves to learn about the Bible and consistently attends a Bible study group each week. Her friend Hannah has started bringing two girls to the group and to church on Sundays. Jobee knows these girls, and she knows they have reputations for the wild life—partying, drinking, and guys.

At first Jobee was a little disappointed that Hannah's friends had "interrupted" the Bible study, but later she was glad that they were curious about Jesus. After a few weeks, both girls said they wanted to change their ways and get right with God. One night after the Bible study, they both did so. Jobee felt a sense of pride that these two girls fell in love with Jesus at her Bible study.

One Friday night while at Hannah's birthday party, the two girls came late…and drunk. They denied it, but it was obvious. They left Hannah's house and walked to a rowdy party down the street flowing with alcohol. Jobee was furious. She thought that they were serious about their commitment to God and his ways. *Were they lying or just faking it?* she wondered.

When Jobee saw them at church two days later, she was angry. She couldn't believe they showed up at church after getting drunk a few nights before! She ignored them that morning and couldn't shake the feeling that they were total hypocrites.

Jobee, like many of us, needs to be reminded that people are complicated—especially new Christians. Many of us come from painful, difficult pasts, and a new commitment to follow God's ways is just the beginning of a long process. While it's a lot easier to share God's love with people who look and act like us, that wasn't Jesus' way. He singled out the messed up, the immoral, and those rejected by the righteous. Ironically, these people seemed to appreciate Jesus most of all. That's what this session is about.

FELLOWSHIP: CONNECTING YOUR HEART TO OTHERS'

Goal: To share about your life and listen attentively to others, caring about what they share

Here are three options for your opening time. Choose one that will get your group talking.

1. Based on the story that opens this chapter, are you more like Jobee or the two party girls? Why?

2. Which of the previous five sessions have been the most helpful to you? Why?

    - Session 1:   The Father's Heart
    - Session 2:   Jesus in Flesh and Blood
    - Session 3:   Sowing Seeds
    - Session 4:   Who Is My Neighbor?
    - Session 5:   Teaming Up

3. Share one highlight you've experienced with a non-Christian while working through this book.

DISCIPLESHIP: GROWING TO BE LIKE JESUS

Goal: To explore God's Word, gain biblical knowledge, and make personal applications

People in pain often show obvious signs that they need God's help. People hide their pain in many different ways—they may live wild lifestyles, party, drink, swear, have sex, gossip, fight, and the like.

It can be easy to look at people like this and think, *Oh, they're jerks. They're losers.* It's easy to blow them off and ignore their signs of brokenness. But Jesus watched for those signs and responded to the need he saw. He did that with Zacchaeus. This may be a familiar passage to you, but try to see it in new ways as you learn to look out for those who hurt deeply.

Read Luke 19:1-10. (If you don't have a Bible, the passage is on page 97.)

1. What do you think motivated Zacchaeus to see Jesus?

2. Zacchaeus had a lot to overcome in order to connect with Jesus. What are some of the common barriers that keep hurting people from connecting with Jesus?

3. Why do you think Jesus didn't mind shocking people when he invited himself to Zacchaeus' home?

4. What kinds of people do Christians tend to look down upon—even if it's an unspoken distaste?

5. The crowd judged Zacchaeus, looking down on him and labeling his heart. Do you ever find yourself being too judgmental? When?

6. How often do others' opinions negatively affect the way you live out your faith? Explain your answer.

7. What was Zacchaeus' attitude toward wealth? Do you ever find yourself getting caught up in things that appear more important than God? If so, what are they?

8. What can you do about people like Zacchaeus, who live in your world and are disliked by many Christians? Who are they, and how might you help them?

9. Jesus made a strong statement about his life mission in verse 10. In what ways is your life mission similar or different?

EVANGELISM: SHARING YOUR STORY AND GOD'S STORY

Goal: To consider how the truths from this session might be applied to your relationships with unbelievers

1. When you think about spending time among the broken people in your world—the people like Zacchaeus—which (if any) of the following concerns do you struggle with?

   - Being viewed as "one of them"
   - Exposing my own less-than-perfect Christian life
   - Exposing myself to people with really bad habits
   - Appearing to support their sin and lifestyles
   - Getting in trouble with my parents because I hang out with "those types"
   - Being judged by Christian friends for associating with "those types"
   - Other:

MINISTRY: SERVING OTHERS IN LOVE

Goal: To recognize and take advantage of opportunities to serve others

We hope that by this last session you have learned more about the close connection between evangelism and ministry. While they are unique and have different biblical purposes, there is a close connection between caring for people (ministry) and sharing the good news of God's love story (evangelism) with them. Evangelism often happens most effectively as a result of meeting someone's needs *first* and sharing Jesus *second*.

1. As a group, discuss the connection between ministry and evangelism and then personalize it. Answer this question: How are you currently being evangelistic through your acts of ministry?

2. If you were forced to give yourself a letter grade based on the biblical purposes of evangelism and ministry, which would get the A-grade and which would get the B-grade? Explain why. (In other words, which one comes more naturally to you?)

Since this is the last time your group will be together with this particular book as your guide, make sure you take some time to discuss what will happen to your group next. If you want to continue to study the incredible life and teachings of Jesus, there are a total of six books in this series.

WORSHIP: SURRENDERING YOUR LIFE TO HONOR GOD

Goal: To consider how the truths from this session might be applied to your relationships with unbelievers

As you finish this study of evangelism, use this time to prayerfully summarize some key things you've learned and experienced throughout this book. Go around the group and have each person pray for one of the following (if your group is small, you may need to double-up your prayers; if it's larger, you may need to add more items to pray for):

- Pray for sensitivity to listen to others' stories.
- Pray for opportunities to share your story (testimony).
- Pray for wisdom to know more of God's love story for others.

- Pray for awareness to plant spiritual seeds when opportunities arise.
- Pray for open eyes to meet people's needs through ministry.
- Pray for God to give you a friend with whom you can share in the joy of being an evangelistic partner.
- Pray for those who are lost and hurting.
- Pray for those in your group who are going to lead others through one of the other Jesus books in this series.

AT HOME THIS WEEK

Option 1: A Weekly Reflection

Take another self-evaluation that reflects five areas of your spiritual life (fellowship, discipleship, ministry, evangelism, and worship). See pages 84-85.

Option 2: Daily Bible Readings

Check out the Bible reading plan on pages 114-115.

Option 3: Memory Verses

Memorize another verse from pages 119-120.

Option 4: Journaling

Choose one or more of the following options:

- Write down whatever is on your mind.
- Read your journal entry from last week and write a reflection about it.
- Complete these statements: Sharing my story requires me to… Listening to others' stories requires me to… Revealing God's story requires me to…

Option 5: Wrap It Up

Write out your answers to any questions that you didn't answer during your small group time.

LEARN A LITTLE MORE

He wanted to see Jesus (Luke 19:3)

The disciples often saw people like Zacchaeus as distractions rather than opportunities to extend love (Matthew 15:23,32-33). But Jesus regularly reminded them that people were the mission, not the distraction.

I will pay back four times the amount (19:8)

Paying back four times the amount was far more than the Old Testament required (Leviticus 5:16, Numbers 5:7). Zacchaeus may have really gouged people for money, or he may have wanted to show his great repentance and new devotion to Jesus. True repentance (like Zacchaeus') always results in a changed lifestyle. One specific change is seeking to make things right with others we have wronged.

FOR DEEPER STUDY ON YOUR OWN

1. To get a better picture of the kinds of people Jesus hung out with, check out the following passages: Matthew 9:9-17, 11:16-19; Luke 15:1-3.

2. Our past doesn't keep us from God's love. Read about his unconditional love for us in Ephesians 2:1-10 and Titus 3:4-8.

3. How did Paul address the fear in 2 Corinthians 4:5-12 that our less-than-perfect lives make us bad witnesses for Jesus?

4. Read Luke 5:27-32. With his limited time on earth, Jesus made the "sick" a priority over the "healthy." To what extent do you think that's a good model for you? How much time do you need to spend with the "healthy" and why? Why do you think Jesus didn't worry about appearing to condone sin when he dined with sinners?

A WEEKLY REFLECTION

Take a minute to reflect on how well you've been doing in the following five areas of your spiritual life this week—a 10 means you did an amazing job. This reflection can serve as a spiritual gauge to help you consider some very important areas. This is for your personal evaluation and growth; it's NOT a test—no one else needs to see it.

FELLOWSHIP: CONNECTING YOUR HEART TO OTHERS

How well did I connect with other Christians?

1   2   3   4   5   6   7   8   9   10

DISCIPLESHIP: GROWING TO BE LIKE JESUS

How well did I take steps to grow spiritually and deepen my faith on my own?

1   2   3   4   5   6   7   8   9   10

MINISTRY: SERVING OTHERS IN LOVE

How well did I recognize opportunities to serve others and follow through?

1   2   3   4   5   6   7   8   9   10

EVANGELISM: SHARING YOUR STORY AND GOD'S STORY

How well did I engage in spiritual conversations with non-Christians?

1   2   3   4   5   6   7   8   9   10

WORSHIP: SURRENDERING YOUR LIFE TO HONOR GOD

How well did I focus on God's presence and honor him with my life? Was my relationship with God a primary focus?

1   2   3   4   5   6   7   8   9   10

When you finish, celebrate the areas where you feel good and consider how you can use those strengths to help others in their journey to be more like Jesus. You might also want to take time to identify some potential areas for growth.

APPENDICES

SMALL GROUP LEADER CHECKLIST

- Read through "For Small Group Leaders: How to Best Use this Material" (see pages 89-92). This is very important—familiarizing yourself with it will help you understand content and how to best manage your time.

- **Read through all the questions in the session that you'll be leading.** The questions are a guide for you to help students grow spiritually. Think through which questions are best for your group. Remember, no curriculum author knows your students better than you do! Just a small amount of preparation on your part will help you manage the time you'll have with your group. Based on the amount of time you'll have in your small group, circle the questions you will discuss as a group. Decide what (if anything) you will assign at the end of the session (things like homework, snacks, group project, and so on).

- **Remember that the questions in this book don't always have obvious, neat, tidy answers.** Some are purposely written to cause good discussion without a specific "right" answer. Often questions (and answers) will lead to more questions.

- **Make sure you have enough books for your students and a few extra in case your students invite friends.** (Note: It's vital for your group to decide during the first session whether you can invite friends to join your group. If not, encourage your group to think of friends they can invite if you go through the next EXPERIENCING CHRIST TOGETHER book in this series.)

- **Read the material included in this appendix.** It's filled with information that will benefit your group and your student ministry. This appendix alone is a great reference for students—familiarize yourself with the tools here so you can offer them to students.

- **Submit your leadership and your group to God.** Ask God to provide you with insight into how to lead your group, patience to do so, and courage to speak truth in love when needed.

FOR SMALL GROUP LEADERS: HOW TO BEST USE THIS MATERIAL

This book was written more as a guidebook than a workbook. In most workbooks, you're supposed to answer every question and fill in all the blanks. In this book, there are lots of questions and plenty of blank space. Explain to your students that this isn't a school workbook—they're not graded on how much they've written.

The number-one rule for this curriculum is that there are no rules apart from the ones you decide to use. Every small group is unique and will figure out its own style and system. (The exception is when the lead youth worker establishes a guideline for all the groups to follow. In that case, respect your leader's guidelines.)

If you need a guide to get you started until you navigate your own way, here's a way to adapt the material for a 60-minute session.

Introduction (4 minutes)

Begin each session with one student reading the Small Group Covenant (see page 18). This becomes a constant reminder of why you'll be doing what you're doing. Then have another student read the opening paragraphs of the session you'll be discussing. Allow different students to take turns reading these two opening pieces.

Connecting (10 minutes)

This section can take 45 minutes if you're not careful! You'll need to stay on task to keep this segment short—consider giving students a specific amount of time and holding them to it. It's always better to leave students wanting more time for discussion than to leave them bored.

Growing (25 minutes)

Read God's Word and work through the questions you think will be best for your group. This section definitely has more questions than you're able to discuss in the allotted time. Before the small group begins, take some time to read through the questions and choose the best ones for your group. You may also want to add questions of your own. If someone forgets a Bible, we've provided the Scripture passages for each session in the appendix.

The questions in this book don't always have obvious, neat, tidy answers. Some are purposely written to cause good discussion without a specific "right" answer. Often questions (and answers) will lead to more questions.

If your small group is biblically mature, this section won't be too difficult. However, if your group struggles with these questions, make sure you sift through them and focus on the few questions that will help drive the message home. Also, you might want to encourage your group to answer the remaining questions on their own.

Serving and Sharing (10 minutes)

If you're pressed for time, you may choose to skip one of these two sections. If you do need to skip one due to time constraints, group members can finish the section on their own during the week. Don't feel guilty about passing over a section. **One of the strengths of this material is the built-in, intentional repetition in every session. You will have other opportunities to discuss that biblical purpose.** (Again, that's the main reason for spending a few minutes before your group meets to read through all the questions and pick the best ones for your group.)

Surrendering (10 minutes)

We always want to end the lesson with a focus on God and a specific time of prayer. You'll have several options but feel free to default to your group's comfort level.

Closing Challenge (1 minute)

Encourage students to pick one option each from the "At Home This Week" section to complete on their own. The more students initiate and develop the habit of spending time with God, the healthier their spiritual journeys will be. We've found that students have plenty of unanswered questions that they will consider on their own time. **Keep in mind that the main goal of this book is building spiritual growth in community—not to get your students to answer every question correctly.** Remember that this is your small group, your time, and the questions will always be there. Use them, ignore them, or assign them for personal study during the week—but don't feel pressure to follow this curriculum exactly or "grade" your group's biblical knowledge.

Finally, remember that questions are a great way to get students connected to one another and God's Word. You don't have to have all the answers.

Suggestions for Existing Small Groups

If your small group has been meeting for a while, and you've already established comfortable relationships, you can jump right into the material. But make sure you take the following actions, even if you're a well-established group:

- Read through the "Small Group Covenant" on page 18 and make additions or adjustments as necessary.

- Read the "Prayer Request Guidelines" together (pages 132-133). You can maximize the group's time by following them.

- Before each meeting, consider whether you'll assign material to be completed (or at least thought through) before your next meeting.

- Familiarize yourself with all the "At Home This Week" options at the end of each session. They are explained in detail near the end of Session 1 (page 26), and then briefly summarized at the end of the other five sessions.

Although handling business like this can seem cumbersome or unnecessary to an existing group, these foundational steps can save you from headaches later on because you took the time to create an environment conducive to establishing deep relationships.

Suggestions for New Small Groups

If your group is meeting together for the first time, jumping right into the first session may not be your best option. You may want to meet as a group before you begin going through the book so you can get to know each other better. To prepare for the first gathering, read and follow the "Suggestions for Existing Groups" mentioned previously.

Spend some time getting to know each other with icebreaker questions. Several are listed here. Pick one or two that will work best for your group or use your own. The goal is to break ground so you can plant the seeds of healthy relationships.

1. What's your name, school, grade, and favorite class in school? (Picking your least favorite class is too easy.)

2. Tell the group a brief (basic) history of your family. What's your family life like? How many brothers and sisters do you have? Which family members are you closest to?

3. What's one thing about yourself that you really like?

4. Everyone has little personality quirks—traits that make each one of us unique. What are yours?

5. Why did you choose to be a part of this small group?

6. What do you hope to get out of this small group? How do you expect it to help you?

7. What do you think it will take to make our small group work well?

Need some teaching help?

Companion DVDs are available for each EXPERIENCING CHRIST TOGETHER book. These DVDs contain teaching segments you can use to supplement each session. Play them before your discussion begins or just prior to the "Discipleship" section in each session. The DVDs aren't required, but they are a great complement and supplement to the small group material. These are available from www.youthspecialties.com.

SCRIPTURE PASSAGES

Session 1

Luke 15:1-10

[1]Now the tax collectors and "sinners" were all gathering around to hear him. [2]But the Pharisees and the teachers of the law muttered, "This man welcomes sinners and eats with them."

[3]Then Jesus told them this parable: [4]"Suppose one of you has a hundred sheep and loses one of them. Does he not leave the ninety-nine in the open country and go after the lost sheep until he finds it? [5]And when he finds it, he joyfully puts it on his shoulders [6]and goes home. Then he calls his friends and neighbors together and says, 'Rejoice with me; I have found my lost sheep.' [7]I tell you that in the same way there will be more rejoicing in heaven over one sinner who repents than over ninety-nine righteous persons who do not need to repent.

[8]"Or suppose a woman has ten silver coins and loses one. Does she not light a lamp, sweep the house and search carefully until she finds it? [9]And when she finds it, she calls her friends and neighbors together and says, 'Rejoice with me; I have found my lost coin.' [10]In the same way, I tell you, there is rejoicing in the presence of the angels of God over one sinner who repents."

Session 2

John 1:1-14

[1]In the beginning was the Word, and the Word was with God, and the Word was God. [2]He was with God in the beginning.

[3]Through him all things were made; without him nothing was made that has been made. [4]In him was life, and that life was the light of men. [5]The light shines in the darkness, but the darkness has not understood it.

[6]There came a man who was sent from God; his name was John. [7]He came as a witness to testify concerning that light, so that through him all men might believe. [8]He himself was not the light; he came only as a witness to the light. [9]The true light that gives light to every man was coming into the world.

¹⁰He was in the world, and though the world was made through him, the world did not recognize him. ¹¹He came to that which was his own, but his own did not receive him. ¹²Yet to all who received him, to those who believed in his name, he gave the right to become children of God—¹³children born not of natural descent, nor of human decision or a husband's will, but born of God.

¹⁴The Word became flesh and made his dwelling among us. We have seen his glory, the glory of the One and Only, who came from the Father, full of grace and truth.

Session 3

Matthew 13:1-23

¹That same day Jesus went out of the house and sat by the lake. ²Such large crowds gathered around him that he got into a boat and sat in it, while all the people stood on the shore. ³Then he told them many things in parables, saying: "A farmer went out to sow his seed. ⁴As he was scattering the seed, some fell along the path, and the birds came and ate it up. ⁵Some fell on rocky places, where it did not have much soil. It sprang up quickly, because the soil was shallow. ⁶But when the sun came up, the plants were scorched, and they withered because they had no root. ⁷Other seed fell among thorns, which grew up and choked the plants. ⁸Still other seed fell on good soil, where it produced a crop—a hundred, sixty or thirty times what was sown. ⁹He who has ears let him hear."

¹⁰The disciples came to him and asked, "Why do you speak to the people in parables?"

¹¹He replied, "The knowledge of the secrets of the kingdom of heaven has been given to you, but not to them. ¹²Whoever has will be given more, and he will have an abundance. Whoever does not have, even what he has will be taken from him. ¹³This is why I speak to them in parables:

"Though seeing, they do not see;

   though hearing, they do not hear or understand.

¹⁴In them is fulfilled the prophecy of Isaiah:

"'You will be ever hearing but never understanding;

   you will be ever seeing but never perceiving.

¹⁵For this people's heart has become calloused;

they hardly hear with their ears,

and they have closed their eyes.

Otherwise they might see with their eyes,

hear with their ears,

understand with their hearts and turn,

and I would heal them.'

[16]But blessed are your eyes because they see, and your ears because they hear. [17]For I tell you the truth, many prophets and righteous men longed to see what you see but did not see it, and to hear what you hear but did not hear it.

[18]"Listen then to what the parable of the sower means: [19]When anyone hears the message about the kingdom and does not understand it, the evil one comes and snatches away what was sown in his heart. This is the seed sown along the path. [20]The one who received the seed that fell on rocky places is the man who hears the word and at once receives it with joy. [21]But since he has no root, he lasts only a short time. When trouble or persecution comes because of the word, he quickly falls away. [22]The one who received the seed that fell among the thorns is the man who hears the word, but the worries of this life and the deceitfulness of wealth choke it, making it unfruitful. [23]But the one who received the seed that fell on good soil is the man who hears the word and understands it. He produces a crop, yielding a hundred, sixty or thirty times what was sown."

Session 4

Luke 10:25-37

[25]On one occasion an expert in the law stood up to test Jesus. "Teacher," he asked, "what must I do to inherit eternal life?"

[26]"What is written in the Law?" he replied. "How do you read it?"

[27]He answered: "'Love the Lord your God with all your heart and with all your soul and with all your strength and with all your mind'; and, 'Love your neighbor as yourself.'"

[28]"You have answered correctly," Jesus replied. "Do this and you will live."

²⁹But he wanted to justify himself, so he asked Jesus, "And who is my neighbor?"

³⁰In reply Jesus said: "A man was going down from Jerusalem to Jericho, when he fell into the hands of robbers. They stripped him of his clothes, beat him and went away, leaving him half dead. ³¹A priest happened to be going down the same road, and when he saw the man, he passed by on the other side. ³²So too, a Levite, when he came to the place and saw him, passed by on the other side. ³³But a Samaritan, as he traveled, came where the man was; and when he saw him, he took pity on him. ³⁴He went to him and bandaged his wounds, pouring on oil and wine. Then he put the man on his own donkey, took him to an inn and took care of him. ³⁵The next day he took out two silver coins and gave them to the innkeeper. 'Look after him,' he said, 'and when I return, I will reimburse you for any extra expense you may have.'

³⁶"Which of these three do you think was a neighbor to the man who fell into the hands of robbers?"

³⁷The expert in the law replied, "The one who had mercy on him."

Jesus told him, "Go and do likewise."

Session 5

Luke 10:1-12

¹After this the Lord appointed seventy-two others and sent them two by two ahead of him to every town and place where he was about to go. ²He told them, "The harvest is plentiful, but the workers are few. Ask the Lord of the harvest, therefore, to send out workers into his harvest field. ³Go! I am sending you out like lambs among wolves. ⁴Do not take a purse or bag or sandals; and do not greet anyone on the road.

⁵"When you enter a house, first say, 'Peace to this house.' ⁶If a man of peace is there, your peace will rest on him; if not, it will return to you. ⁷Stay in that house, eating and drinking whatever they give you, for the worker deserves his wages. Do not move around from house to house.

⁸"When you enter a town and are welcomed, eat what is set before you. ⁹Heal the sick who are there and tell them, 'The kingdom of God is near you.' ¹⁰But when you enter a town and are not welcomed, go into its streets and say, ¹¹"Even the dust of your town that sticks to our feet we wipe off against you. Yet be sure of this: The kingdom of God is near.' ¹²I tell you, it will be more bearable on that day for Sodom than for that town."

Session 6

Luke 19:1-10

¹Jesus entered Jericho and was passing through. ²A man was there by the name of Zacchaeus; he was a chief tax collector and was wealthy. ³He wanted to see who Jesus was, but being a short man he could not, because of the crowd. ⁴So he ran ahead and climbed a sycamore-fig tree to see him, since Jesus was coming that way.

⁵When Jesus reached the spot, he looked up and said to him, "Zacchaeus, come down immediately. I must stay at your house today." ⁶So he came down at once and welcomed him gladly.

⁷All the people saw this and began to mutter, "He has gone to be the guest of a 'sinner.'"

⁸But Zacchaeus stood up and said to the Lord, "Look, Lord! Here and now I give half of my possessions to the poor, and if I have cheated anybody out of anything, I will pay back four times the amount."

⁹Jesus said to him, "Today salvation has come to this house, because this man, too, is a son of Abraham. ¹⁰For the Son of Man came to seek and to save what was lost."

WHO IS JESUS?

Jesus is God

The high priest said to him, "I charge you under oath by the living God: Tell us if you are the Christ, the Son of God." "Yes, it is as you say," Jesus replied. (Matthew 26:63-64)

Jesus became a person

The Word [Jesus] became flesh and made his dwelling among us. (John 1:14)

Jesus taught with authority

They were amazed at his teaching, for he taught as one who had real authority—quite unlike the teachers of religious law. (Mark 1:22)

Jesus healed the sick

Jesus went throughout Galilee, teaching in their synagogues, preaching the good news of the kingdom, and healing every disease and sickness among the people. (Matthew 4:23)

Jesus befriended outcasts

That night Matthew invited Jesus and his disciples to be his dinner guests, along with his fellow tax collectors and many other notorious sinners. The Pharisees were indignant. "Why does your teacher eat with such scum?" they asked his disciples. (Matthew 9:10-11)

Jesus got angry with religious oppressors

How terrible it will be for you teachers of religious law and you Pharisees. Hypocrites! You are like whitewashed tombs—beautiful on the outside but filled on the inside with dead people's bones and all sorts of impurity. (Matthew 23:27)

Jesus was persecuted

The chief priests and the whole Sanhedrin were looking for false evidence against Jesus so that they could put him to death. But they did not find any, though many false witnesses came forward. Finally two came forward. (Matthew 26:59-60)

Jesus was tempted in every way

… for he [Jesus] faced all of the same temptations we do… (Hebrews 4:15)

Jesus never sinned

… he [Jesus] did not sin. (Hebrews 4:15)

But you know that he [Jesus] appeared so that he might take away our sins. And in him is no sin. (1 John 3:5)

Jesus died, rose from the dead, and continues to live to this day

But Christ has indeed been raised from the dead… (1 Corinthians 15:20)

Jesus made it possible to have a relationship with God

For God so loved the world that he gave his one and only Son, that whoever believes in him shall not perish but have eternal life. For God did not send his Son into the world to condemn the world, but to save the world through him. (John 3:16-17)

Jesus can sympathize with our struggles

This High Priest of ours understands our weaknesses… (Hebrews 4:15)

Jesus loves us

May you experience the love of Christ, though it is so great you will never fully understand it. (Ephesians 3:19)

Sound good? Looking for more?

Getting to know Jesus is the best thing you can do with your life. He WON'T let you down. He knows everything about you and LOVES you more than you can imagine!

A SUMMARY OF THE LIFE OF JESUS

The Incarnation

Fully divine and fully human, God sent his son, Jesus, to the earth to bring salvation into the world for everyone who believes. *Read John 1:4.*

John the Baptist

A relative to Jesus, John was sent "to make ready a people prepared for the Lord." He called Israel to repentance and baptized people in the Jordan River. *Read Luke 3:3.*

The baptism and temptation of Jesus

After John baptized him, Jesus went into the desert for 40 days in preparation for his ministry. He faced Satan and resisted the temptation he offered by quoting Scripture. *Read Matthew 4:4.*

Jesus begins his ministry

The world's most influential person taught with authority, healed with compassion, and inspired with miracles. *Read Luke 4:15.*

Jesus' model of discipleship

Jesus called everyone to follow him—without reservation—and to love God and others. *Read Luke 9:23, 57-62.*

The opposition

The religious "upper class" opposed Jesus, seeking to discredit him in the eyes of the people. Jesus criticized their hypocrisy and love of recognition. *Read Matthew 23:25.*

The great "I Am"

Jesus claimed to be the bread of life; the light of the world; the good shepherd; and the way, the truth, and the life. Each of these titles reveals essential truth about who he is. *Read John 14:6.*

The great physician

His words brought conviction and comfort; his actions shouted to the world his true nature. Healing the sick, Jesus demonstrated his power and authority by helping people where they needed it most so they might accept the truth. *Read Matthew 14:14.*

The great forgiver

Humanity's deepest need is forgiveness and freedom from the guilt of the past—which separates us from God. Only God has the power to forgive, and Jesus further demonstrated his divinity by forgiving the guilty. *Read Matthew 9:6.*

The disciples

Jesus chose 12 ordinary men to change the world. They weren't rich, powerful, or influential. They had shady pasts, often made huge mistakes, and were filled with doubts. In spite of these things, Jesus used them to build his church. *Read Mark 3:14.*

The final night

On the night before his death, Jesus spent the time preparing his disciples, and he spent time alone. Obedient to the Father, Jesus was committed to go to the cross to pay the penalty for our sins. *Read Mark 14:32 ff.*

The Crucifixion

Jesus died a real death on the cross for the sins of the world. His ultimate sacrifice is something all believers should remember often. *Read John 19:30.*

The Resurrection

After dying on the cross, Jesus was raised from the dead by God's power. This miracle has never been disproved and validates everything Jesus taught. *Read 1 Corinthians 15:55.*

Want a more detailed chronology of Jesus' life and ministry on earth? Check out these two Web sites:

http://www.bookofjesus.com/bojchron.htm and
http://mb-soft.com/believe/txh/gospgosp.htm

SMALL GROUP ROSTER

NAME	E-MAIL	PHONE	ADDRESS / CITY / ZIP CODE	SCHOOL/GRADE

HOW TO KEEP YOUR GROUP FROM BECOMING A CLIQUE

We all want to belong—God created us to be connected in community with one another. But the same drive that creates healthy community can also create negative community, often called a clique. A clique isn't just a group of friends—it's a group of friends uninterested in anyone outside their group. Cliques result in pain for those who are excluded.

If you read the second paragraph of the introduction (page 7), you see the words *spiritual community* used to describe your small group. If your small group becomes a clique, it's an unspiritual community. You have a clique when the biblical purpose of fellowship turns inward. That's ugly. It's the opposite of what God intended the body of Christ to be. Here's why:

- Cliques make your youth ministry look bad.

- Cliques make your small group appear immature.

- Cliques hurt the feelings of excluded people.

- Cliques contradict the value God places on each person.

- Few things are as unappealing as a youth ministry filled with cliques.

Many leaders avoid using their small groups as a way toward spiritual growth because they fear their groups will become cliques. But when they're healthy, small groups can improve your youth ministry's well-being, friendliness, and depth. The apostle Paul reminds us, "Be wise in the way you act toward outsiders; make the most of every opportunity" (Colossians 4:5).

Here are some ideas for being wise and preventing your small group from turning into a clique:

Be Aware

Learn to recognize when outsiders are uncomfortable with your group. It's easy to forget when you're an insider how bad it feels to be an outsider.

Reach Out

Once you're aware of someone feeling left out, make efforts to be friendly. Smile, shake hands, say hello, ask him or her to sit with you or your group, and ask simple yet personal questions. An outsider may come across as defensive, so be as accepting as possible.

Launch New Small Groups

Any small group with the attitude of "us four and no more" has become a clique. A time will come when your small group should launch into multiple small groups if it gets too big—because the bigger a small group gets, the less healthy it becomes. If your small group understands this, you can foster a culture of growth and fellowship.

For Students Only

Small group members expect adult leaders to confront them for acting like a clique. But instead of waiting for an adult to make the move, shock everyone by stepping up and challenging what you know is destructive. Take a risk. Be a spokesperson for your youth ministry and your student peers by leading the way. Be part of a small group that isn't cliquey and don't be afraid to challenge those who are.

SPIRITUAL HEALTH ASSESSMENT

Evaluating your spiritual journey is important—that's why we've encouraged you to take a brief survey at the end of each session. The following few pages are simply longer versions of that short evaluation tool.

Your spiritual journey will take you to low spots as well as high places. Spiritual growth is not a smooth incline—a loopy roller coaster is more like it. When you regularly consider your life, you'll develop an awareness of God's Spirit working in you. Evaluate. Think. Learn. Grow.

The assessment in this section is a tool, not a test. The purpose of this tool is to help you evaluate where you are in your faith journey. No one is perfect, so don't worry about your score. It won't be published in your church bulletin. Be honest so you have an accurate idea of how you're doing.

When you finish, celebrate the areas where you're relatively healthy and think about how you can use your strengths to help others on their spiritual journeys. Then think of ways your group members can help one another to improve weak areas through support and example.

FELLOWSHIP: CONNECTING YOUR HEART TO OTHERS

1. I meet consistently with a small group of Christians.

1	2	3	4	5
POOR				OUTSTANDING

2. I'm connected to other Christians who hold me accountable.

1	2	3	4	5
POOR				OUTSTANDING

3. I can talk with my small group leader when I need help, advice, or support.

1	2	3	4	5
POOR				OUTSTANDING

4. My Christian friends are a significant source of strength and stability in my life.

1	2	3	4	5
POOR				OUTSTANDING

5. I regularly pray for others in my small group outside of our meetings.

1	2	3	4	5
POOR				OUTSTANDING

6. I have resolved all conflicts with other people—both Christians and non-Christians.

1	2	3	4	5
POOR				OUTSTANDING

7. I've done all I possibly can to be a good son or daughter and brother or sister.

1	2	3	4	5
POOR				OUTSTANDING

TOTAL:_____

Take time to answer the following questions to further evaluate your spiritual health. You can do this after your small group meets if you don't have time during the meeting. If you need help with this, schedule a time with your small group leader to talk about your spiritual health.

8. List the three most significant relationships you have right now. Why are these people important to you?

9. How would you describe the benefit from being in fellowship with other Christians?

10. Do you have an accountability partner? If so, what have you been doing to hold each other accountable? If not, how can you get one?

DISCIPLESHIP: GROWING TO BE LIKE JESUS

11. I have regular times of conversation with God.

1	2	3	4	5
POOR				OUTSTANDING

12. I'm closer to God this month than I was last month.

1	2	3	4	5
POOR				OUTSTANDING

13. I'm making better decisions this month compared to last month.

1	2	3	4	5
POOR				OUTSTANDING

14. I regularly attend church services and grow spiritually as a result.

1	2	3	4	5
POOR				OUTSTANDING

15. I consistently honor God with my finances through giving.

1	2	3	4	5
POOR				OUTSTANDING

16. I regularly study the Bible on my own.

1	2	3	4	5
POOR				OUTSTANDING

17. I regularly memorize Bible verses or passages.

1	2	3	4	5
POOR				OUTSTANDING

TOTAL:_____

Take time to answer the following questions to further evaluate your spiritual health. You can do this after your small group meets if you don't have time during the meeting. If you need help with this, schedule a time with your small group leader to talk about your spiritual health.

18. What books or chapters from the Bible have you read during the last month?

19. What has God been teaching you lately from Scripture?

20. What was the last verse you memorized? When did you memorize it? Describe the last time a memorized Bible verse helped you.

MINISTRY: SERVING OTHERS IN LOVE

21. I am currently serving in some ministry capacity.

1	2	3	4	5
POOR				OUTSTANDING

22. I'm effectively ministering where I'm serving.

1	2	3	4	5
POOR				OUTSTANDING

23. Generally I have a humble attitude when I serve others.

1	2	3	4	5
POOR				OUTSTANDING

24. I understand God has created me as a unique individual, and he has a special plan for my life.

1	2	3	4	5
POOR				OUTSTANDING

25. When I help others, I typically don't look for anything in return.

1	2	3	4	5
POOR				OUTSTANDING

26. My family and friends consider me generally unselfish.

1	2	3	4	5
POOR				OUTSTANDING

27. I'm usually sensitive to others' hurts and respond in a caring way.

1	2	3	4	5
POOR				OUTSTANDING

TOTAL:_____

Take time to answer the following questions to further evaluate your spiritual health. You can do this after your small group meets if you don't have time during the meeting. If you need help with this, schedule a time with your small group leader to talk about your spiritual health.

28. If you're currently serving in a ministry, why are you serving? If not, what's kept you from getting involved?

29. What spiritual lessons have you learned while serving?

30. What frustrations have you experienced as a result of serving?

EVANGELISM: SHARING YOUR STORY AND GOD'S STORY

31. I regularly pray for my non-Christian friends.

1	2	3	4	5
POOR				OUTSTANDING

32. I invite my non-Christian friends to church.

1	2	3	4	5
POOR				OUTSTANDING

33. I talk about my faith with others.

1	2	3	4	5
POOR				OUTSTANDING

34. I pray for opportunities to share what Jesus has done in my life.

1	2	3	4	5
POOR				OUTSTANDING

35. People know I'm a Christian because of what I do, not just because of what I say.

1	2	3	4	5
POOR				OUTSTANDING

36. I feel strong compassion for non-Christians.

1	2	3	4	5
POOR				OUTSTANDING

37. I have written my testimony and am ready to share it.

1	2	3	4	5
POOR				OUTSTANDING

TOTAL:_____

Take time to answer the following questions to further evaluate your spiritual health. You can do this after your small group meets if you don't have time during the meeting. If you need help with this, schedule a time with your small group leader to talk about your spiritual health.

38. Describe any significant spiritual conversations you've had with non-Christians during the last month.

39. Have non-Christians ever challenged your faith? If yes, describe how.

40. Describe some difficulties you've faced when sharing your faith.

41. What successes have you experienced recently in personal evangelism? (Success isn't limited to bringing people to salvation directly. Helping someone take a step closer at any point on his or her spiritual journey is success.)

WORSHIP: SURRENDERING YOUR LIFE TO HONOR GOD

42. I consistently participate in Sunday and midweek worship experiences at church.

1	2	3	4	5
POOR				OUTSTANDING

43. My heart breaks over the things that break God's heart.

1	2	3	4	5
POOR				OUTSTANDING

44. I regularly give thanks to God.

1	2	3	4	5
POOR				OUTSTANDING

45. I'm living a life that, overall, honors God.

1	2	3	4	5
POOR				OUTSTANDING

46. I have an attitude of wonder and awe toward God.

1	2	3	4	5
POOR				OUTSTANDING

47. I often use the free access I have into God's presence.

1	2	3	4	5
POOR				OUTSTANDING

TOTAL:_____

Take time to answer the following questions to further evaluate your spiritual health. You can do this after your small group meets if you don't have time during the meeting. If you need help with this, schedule a time with your small group leader to talk about your spiritual health.

48. Make a list of your top five priorities. You can get a good idea of your priorities by evaluating how you spend your time. Be realistic and honest. Are your priorities are in the right order? Do you need to get rid of some or add new priorities? (As a student you may have some limitations. This isn't ammo for dropping out of school or disobeying parents!)

49. List 10 things you're thankful for.

50. What influences, directs, guides, or controls you the most?

DAILY BIBLE READINGS

As you meet with your small group for Bible study, prayer, and encouragement, you'll grow spiritually. But no matter how wonderful your small group experience, you need to learn to grow spiritually on your own, too. God has given you an incredible tool to help—his love letter, the Bible. The Bible reveals God's love for you and gives directions for living life to the fullest.

To help you with this, we've included a fairly easy way to read through a section of the Bible. Instead of feeling like you need to sit down and read the entire book at once, we've broken down the reading into bite-size chunks. Check off the passages as you read them. Don't feel guilty if you miss a daily reading. Simply do your best to develop the habit of being in God's Word daily.

A 36-Day Journey Through Paul's Writings

Imagine sitting at the feet of Paul: the apostle who began his spiritual career as a pharisee and zealous persecutor of Christians and ended it as the greatest evangelist and church planter of the Christian faith. Like the members of the churches he founded 2,000 years ago, you can read Paul's words of encouragement and instruction today and learn, as he did, to pattern your life after the Savior who changed his life on the Road to Damascus.

Day 1	Galatians 1
Day 2	Galatians 2
Day 3	Galatians 3
Day 4	Galatians 4
Day 5	Galatians 5
Day 6	Galatians 6
Day 7	Ephesians 1
Day 8	Ephesians 2
Day 9	Ephesians 3
Day 10	Ephesians 4
Day 11	Ephesians 5
Day 12	Ephesians 6

HOW TO STUDY THE BIBLE ON YOUR OWN

The Bible is the foundation for all the books in the EXPERIENCING CHRIST TOGETHER series. Every lesson contains a Bible passage for your small group to study and apply. To maximize the impact of your small group experience, it's helpful if each participant spends time reading and studying the Bible during the week. When you read the Bible for yourself, you can have discussions based on what *you* know the Bible says instead of what another member has heard second- or third-hand about the Bible.

Growing Christians learn to study the Bible so they can grow spiritually on their own. Here are some principles about studying the Bible to help you give God's Word a central place in your life.

Choose a Time and Place

Since we are easily distracted, pick a time when you're at your best. If you're a morning person, then study the Bible in the morning. Find a place away from phones, computers, and TVs so you are less likely to be interrupted.

Begin with Prayer

Acknowledge God's presence with you. Thank him for his gifts, confess your sins, and ask for his guidance and understanding as you study his love letter to you.

Start with Excitement

We often take God's Word for granted and forget what an incredible gift we have. God wasn't forced to reach out to us, but he did. He's made it possible for us to know him, understand his directions, and be encouraged—all through his Word, the Bible. Remind yourself how amazing it is that God wants you to know him.

Read the Passage

After choosing a passage, read it several times. You might want to read it slowly, pausing after each sentence. If possible, read it out loud. (Remember that before the Bible was written on paper, it was spoken verbally from generation to generation.)

Keep a Journal

Respond to God's Word by writing down how you're challenged, truths to remember, thanksgiving and praise, sins to confess, commands to obey, or any other thoughts you have.

Dig Deep

When you read the Bible, look deeper than the plain meaning of the words. Here are a few ideas about what to look for:

- *Truth about God's character.* What do the verses reveal about God's character?

- *Truth about your life and our world.* You don't have to figure out life on your own. Life can be difficult, but when you know how the world works, you can make good decisions guided by wisdom from God.

- *Truth about the world's past.* The Bible reveals God's intervention in our mistakes and triumphs throughout history. The choices we read about—good and bad—serve as examples to challenge us to greater faith and obedience. (See Hebrews 11:1-12:1.)

- *Truth about our actions.* God will never leave you stranded. Although he allows us all to go through hard times, he is always with us. Our actions have consequences and rewards. Just like he does in Bible stories, God can use all of the consequences and rewards caused by our actions to help others.

As you read, ask these four questions to help you learn from the Bible:

- What do these verses teach me about who God is, how he acts, and how people respond?

- What does this passage teach about the nature of the world?

- What wisdom can I learn from what I read?

- How should I change my life because of what I learned from these verses?

Ask Questions

You may be tempted to skip over parts you don't understand, but don't give up too easily. Understanding the Bible can be hard work. If you come across a word you don't know, look it up in a regular dictionary or a Bible dictionary. If you come across a verse that seems to contradict another verse, see whether your Bible has any notes to explain it. Write down your questions and ask someone who has more knowledge about the Bible than you. Buy or borrow a study Bible or check the Internet. Try *www.gotquestions.org* or *www.carm.org* for answers to your questions.

Apply the Truth to Your Life

The Bible should make a difference in your life. It contains the help you need to live the life God intended. Knowledge of the Bible without personal obedience is worthless and causes hypocrisy and pride. Take time to consider the condition of your thinking, attitudes, and actions, and wonder about how God is working in you. Think about your life situation and how you can serve others better.

More Helpful Ideas

- Decide that the time you have set aside for Bible reading and study is nonnegotiable. Don't let other activities squeeze Bible study time out of your schedule.

- Avoid the extremes of being ritualistic (reading a chapter just to mark it off a list) and being lazy (giving up).

- Begin with realistic goals and boundaries for your study time. If five to seven minutes a day proves a challenge at the beginning, make it a goal to start smaller and increase your time slowly. Don't set yourself up to fail.

- Be open to the leading and teaching of God's Spirit.

- Love God like he's the best friend you'll ever have—which is the truth!

MEMORY VERSES

The word *memory* may cause some of you to groan. In school, you have to memorize dates, places, times, and outcomes. Now you have to memorize the Bible?

No, not the entire Bible! Start small with some key verses. Trust us, this is important. Here's why: Scripture memorization is a good habit for a growing Christian to develop because when God's Word is planted in your mind and heart, it has a way of influencing how you live. King David understood this: "I have hidden your word in my heart that I might not sin against you" (Psalm 119:11).

Challenge one another in your small group to memorize the six verses below—one for each time your small group meets. Hold each other accountable by asking about one another's progress. Write the verses on index cards and keep them handy so you can learn and review them when you have a free moment (standing in line, before class starts, sitting at a red light, when you've finished a test and others are still working, waiting for your dad to get out of the bathroom—you get the picture). You'll be surprised at how many verses you can memorize as you work toward this goal and add verses to your list.

"STARTING A QUARREL IS LIKE BREACHING A DAM; SO DROP THE MATTER BEFORE A DISPUTE BREAKS OUT." —PROVERBS 17:14

"I WRITE THESE THINGS TO YOU WHO BELIEVE IN THE NAME OF THE SON OF GOD SO THAT YOU MAY KNOW THAT YOU HAVE ETERNAL LIFE." —1 JOHN 5:13

"THE LORD IS NOT SLOW IN KEEPING HIS PROMISE, AS SOME UNDERSTAND SLOWNESS. HE IS PATIENT WITH YOU, NOT WANTING ANYONE TO PERISH, BUT EVERYONE TO COME TO REPENTANCE." —2 PETER 3:9

"BUT YOU WILL RECEIVE POWER WHEN THE HOLY SPIRIT COMES ON YOU; AND YOU WILL BE MY WITNESSES IN JERUSALEM, AND IN ALL JUDEA AND SAMARIA, AND TO THE ENDS OF THE EARTH." —ACTS 1:8

"LIVE WISELY AMONG THOSE WHO ARE NOT BELIEVERS, AND MAKE THE MOST OF EVERY OPPORTUNITY." —COLOSSIANS 4:5 NLT

"IN THE SAME WAY, LET YOUR LIGHT SHINE BEFORE MEN, THAT THEY MAY SEE YOUR GOOD DEEDS AND PRAISE YOUR FATHER IN HEAVEN." —MATTHEW 5:16

JOURNALING: SNAPSHOTS OF YOUR HEART

In the simplest terms, journaling is reflection with pen in hand. A growing life needs time to reflect, so several times throughout this book you're asked to journal. In addition, you always have a journaling option at the end of each session. Through these writing opportunities, you're getting a taste of what it means to journal.

When you take time to write your thoughts in a journal, you'll experience many benefits. A journal is more than a diary—it's a series of snapshots of your heart. The goal of journaling is to slow down your life to capture some of the great, crazy, wonderful, chaotic, painful, encouraging, angering, confusing, joyful, and loving thoughts, feelings, and ideas in your life. Keeping a journal can become a powerful habit when you reflect on your life and how God is working in it.

Personal Insights

When confusion abounds in your life, disorderly thoughts and feelings often loom just out of range, slightly out of focus. Putting these thoughts and feelings on paper is like corralling and domesticating wild beasts. Once on paper, you can look at them, consider them, contemplate the reasons they were causing you pain, and learn from them.

Have you ever had trouble answering the question, "How do you feel?" Journaling compels you to become more specific with your generalized thoughts and feelings. This is not to suggest that a page full of words perfectly represents what's happening on the inside. That would be foolish. But journaling can move you closer to understanding more about yourself.

Reflection and Examination

With journaling, you can write about your feelings, your situations, how you responded to events. You can reflect and answer questions like these:

- Was that the right response?

- What were my other options?

- Did I lose control and act impulsively?

- If this happened again, should I do the same thing? Would I do the same thing?

- How can I be different as a result of this situation?

Spiritual Insights

One of the main goals of journaling is to gain new spiritual insights about God, yourself, and the world. When you take time to journal, you have the opportunity to pause and consider how God is working in your life and in the lives of those around you. Journaling helps you see the work he's accomplishing and remember it for the future.

What to Write About

There isn't one right way to journal, no set number of times per week, no rules for the length of each journal entry. Figure out what works best for you. Get started with these options:

Write a letter or prayer to God

Many Christians struggle with maintaining a consistent prayer life. Writing out your prayers can help strengthen it. Begin with this question: "What do I want to tell God right now?"

Write a letter or conversation to another person

Sometimes conversations with others can be difficult because we're not sure what we ought to say. Have you ever walked away from an interaction and 20 minutes later thought, *I should have said...*? Journaling conversations before they happen can help you think through the issues and approach your interactions with others in intentional ways. As a result, you can feel confident as you begin your conversations because you've taken time to consider the issues beforehand.

Process conflict and pain

You may find it helpful to write about your conflicts with others, especially those that take you by surprise. By journaling soon after conflict occurs, you can reflect and learn from it. You'll be better prepared for the next time you face a similar situation. Conflicts are generally difficult to navigate. Thinking through and writing about specific conflicts typically yields helpful personal insights.

When you're experiencing pain is also a good time to settle your thoughts and consider the nature of your feelings. The great thing about exploring your feelings is that you're only accountable to God. You don't have to worry about hurting anyone's feelings by what you write in your journal (if you keep it private).

Examine your motives

The Bible is clear regarding two heart truths. First, how you behave reflects who you are on the inside (Luke 6:45). Second, you can take the right action for the wrong reason (James 4:3).

The condition of your heart is vitally important. Molding your motives to God's desires is central to following Christ. The Pharisees did many of the right things, but for the wrong reasons. Reflect on the *real* reasons why you do what you do.

Anticipate your actions

Have you ever gone to bed thinking, *That was a mistake. I didn't intend that to happen!* Probably! No one is perfect. You can't predict all of the consequences of your actions. But reflecting on how your actions could affect others will guide you and help you relate better to others.

Reflect on God's work in your life

If you journal in the evening, you can answer this question: "What did God teach me today?"

If you journal in the morning, you can answer this question: "God, what were you trying to teach me yesterday that I missed?" When you reflect on yesterday's events, you may find a common theme that God may have been weaving into your life during the day—one you missed because you were busy. When you see God's hand in your life, even a day later, you know God loves you and is guiding you.

Record insights from Scripture

Journal about whatever you learn from the Bible. Rewrite a verse in your own words or figure out how a passage is structured. Try to uncover the key truths from the verses and see how the verses apply to your life. (Again, there is no right way to journal. The only wrong way is to not try it at all.)

JOURNAL PAGES

JOURNAL PAGES

JOURNAL PAGES

JOURNAL PAGES

JOURNAL PAGES

JOURNAL PAGES

PRAYING IN YOUR SMALL GROUP

As believers, we're called to support each other in prayer, and prayer should be a consistent part of a healthy small group.

One of prayer's purposes is aligning our hearts with God's. By doing this, we can more easily get in touch with what's at the center of God's heart. Prayer shouldn't be a how-well-did-I-do performance or a self-conscious, put-on-the-spot task to fear. Your small group may need time to get comfortable with praying out loud, too. That's okay.

When you do pray, silently or aloud, follow the practical, simple words of Jesus in Matthew 6:

Pray sincerely.

"And when you pray, do not be like the hypocrites, for they love to pray standing in the synagogues and on the street corners to be seen by men. I tell you the truth, they have received their reward in full." (Matthew 6:5)

In the Old Testament, God's people were disciplined prayer warriors. They developed specific prayers to use for every special occasion or need. They had prayers for light and darkness, prayers for fire and rain, prayers for good news and bad. They even had prayers for travel, holidays, holy days, and Sabbath days.

Every day the faithful would stop to pray at 9 a.m., noon, and 3 p.m.—a sort of religious coffee break. Their ritual was impressive, to say the least, but being legalistic had its downside. The proud, self-righteous types would strategically plan their schedules to be in the middle of a crowd when it was time for prayer so everyone could hear them as they prayed loudly. You can see the problem. What was intended to promote spiritual passion became a drama to impress others.

God wants our prayers addressed to him alone. That seems obvious enough, yet how many of us pray wanting to impress our listeners rather than wanting to truly communicate with God? This is the problem if you're prideful like the Pharisees about the excellent quality of your prayers. But it can also be a problem if you're new to prayer and are concerned that you don't know how to "pray right." Don't concern yourself with what others think; just talk to God as if you were sitting in a chair next to him.

Pray simply.

"And when you pray, do not keep on babbling like pagans, for they think they will be heard because of their many words. Do not be like them, for your Father knows what you need before you ask him." (Matthew 6:7-8)

God isn't looking to be dazzled with brilliantly crafted language. Nor is he impressed with lengthy monologues. It's freeing to know that he wants us to keep it simple.

Pray specifically.

"This, then, is how you should pray: 'Our Father in heaven, hallowed be your name, your kingdom come, your will be done on earth as it is in heaven. Give us today our daily bread. Forgive us our debts, as we also have forgiven our debtors. And lead us not into temptation, but deliver us from the evil one." *(Matthew 6:9-13)*

What the church has come to call "The Lord's Prayer" is a model of the kind of brief but specific prayers we may offer anytime, anywhere. Look at some of the specific items mentioned:

- Adoration: "hallowed be your name"

- Provision: "your kingdom come...your will be done...give us today our daily bread"

- Forgiveness: "forgive us our debts"

- Protection: "lead us not into temptation"

PRAYER REQUEST GUIDELINES

Because prayer time is so vital, group members need some basic guidelines for sharing, handling, and praying for prayer requests. Without a commitment from each person to honor these simple suggestions, prayer time can become dominated by one person, an opportunity to gossip, or a never-ending story time. (There are appropriate times to tell personal stories, but this may not be the best time.)

Here are a few suggestions for each group to consider:

Write down prayer requests.

Each small group member should write down every prayer request on the "Prayer Request" pages provided. When you commit to a small group, you're agreeing to be part of the spiritual community, and that includes praying for one another. By keeping track of prayer requests, you can see how God answers them. You'll be amazed at God's power and faithfulness.

As an alternative, one person can record the requests and e-mail them to the rest of the group. If your group chooses this option, safeguard confidentiality. Be sure personal information isn't compromised. Some people share e-mail accounts with parents or siblings. Develop a workable plan for this option.

Give everybody an opportunity to share.

As a group, consider the amount of time remaining and the number of people who still want to share. You won't be able to share every thought or detail about a situation.

Obviously if someone experiences a crisis, you may need to focus exclusively on that group member by giving him or her extended time and focused prayer. (However, true crises are infrequent.)

The leader can limit the time by making a comment such as one of the following:

- We have time for everyone to share one praise or request.

- Simply share what to pray for. We can talk in more detail later.

- We're only going to pray for requests about the people in our group. How can we pray for you specifically?

- We've run out of time to share prayer requests. Take a moment to write down your prayer request and give it to me [or identify another person]. You'll get them by e-mail tomorrow.

Just as people are free to share, they're free to not share.

The goal of a healthy small group should be to create an environment where participants feel comfortable sharing about their lives. Still, not everyone needs to share each week. Here's what I tell my small group:

As a small group we're here to support one another in prayer. This doesn't mean that everyone has to share something. In fact, don't assume you have to share at all. There's no need to make up prayer requests just to have something to say. If you have something you'd like the group to pray for, let us know. If not, that's fine, too.

No gossip allowed.

Don't allow sharing prayer requests to become an excuse for gossip. If you're not part of the problem or solution, consider the information gossip. Share the request without the story behind it—that helps prevent gossip. Also speak in general terms without giving names or details ("I have a friend who's in trouble. God knows who it is. Pray for me that I can be a good friend.").

If a prayer request starts going astray, someone should kindly intercede, perhaps with a question such as, "How can we pray for you in this situation?"

Don't give advice or try to fix the problem.

When people share their struggles and problems, a common response is to try to fix the problem by offering advice. At the right time, the group might provide input on a particular problem, but during prayer time, keep focused on praying for the need. Often God's best work in a person's life comes through times of struggle and pain.

Keep in touch.

Make sure you exchange phone numbers and e-mail addresses before you leave the first meeting. That way you can contact someone who needs prayer or encouragement before the next time your group meets. You can write each person's contact information on the "Small Group Roster" (page 102).

PRAYER OPTIONS

There's no single, correct way to end all your sessions. In addition to the options provided in each session, here are some additional ideas.

During the Small Group Gathering

- One person closes in prayer for the entire group.

- Pray silently. Have one person close the silent prayer time after a while with "amen."

- The leader or another group member prays out loud for each person in the group.

- Everyone prays for one request or person. This can be done randomly during prayer or, as the request is shared, a willing person can announce, "I'll pray for that."

- Everyone who wants to pray takes a turn. Not everyone needs to pray out loud.

- Split the group into half and pray together in smaller groups.

- Pair up and pray for each other.

- On occasion, each person can share what he or she is thankful for before a prayer request, so prayer requests don't become negative from focusing only on problems. Prayer isn't just asking for stuff—it also includes praising God and being thankful for his generosity toward us.

- If you're having an animated discussion about a Bible passage or a life situation, don't feel like you must cut it short for prayer requests. Use it as an opportunity to add a little variety to the prayer time by praying some other day between sessions.

Outside the Group Time

You can use these options if you run out of time to pray during the meeting or in addition to prayer during the meeting.

- Send prayer requests to each other via e-mail.

- Pick prayer partners and phone each other during the week.

- Have each person in the small group choose a day to pray for everyone in the group. Perhaps you can work it out to have each day of the week covered. Let participants report back at each meeting for accountability.

- Have each person pray for just one other person in the group for the entire week. (Everyone prays for the person on the left or on the right or draw names.)

PRAYER REQUEST LOG

DATE | NAME | REQUEST | ANSWER

PRAYER REQUEST LOG

DATE	NAME	REQUEST	ANSWER

PRAYER REQUEST LOG

DATE	NAME	REQUEST	ANSWER

PRAYER REQUEST LOG

DATE

NAME

REQUEST

ANSWER

PRAYER REQUEST LOG

DATE

NAME

REQUEST

ANSWER

PRAYER REQUEST LOG

DATE | NAME | REQUEST | ANSWER

EXPERIENCING CHRIST TOGETHER FOR A YEAR

Your group will benefit the most if you work through the entire EXPE-RIENCING CHRIST TOGETHER series. The longer your group is together, the better your chances of maturing spiritually and integrating the biblical purposes into your life. Here's a plan to complete the series in one year.

Begin with a planning meeting and review the books in the series. They are:

Book 1—Beginning in Jesus: Six Sessions on the Life of Christ

Book 2—Connecting in Jesus: Six Sessions on Fellowship

Book 3—Growing in Jesus: Six Sessions on Discipleship

Book 4—Serving Like Jesus: Six Sessions on Ministry

Book 5—Sharing Jesus: Six Sessions on Evangelism

Book 6—Surrendering to Jesus: Six Sessions on Worship

We recommend you begin with *Book 1—Beginning in Jesus: Six Sessions on the Life of Christ,* because it contains an introduction to six qualities of Jesus. After that, you can use the books in any order that works for your particular ministry.

As you look at your youth ministry calendar, you may want to tailor the order in which you study the books to complement events your youth group will experience. For example, if you plan to have an evangelism outreach, study *Book 5—Sharing Jesus: Six Sessions on Evangelism* first to build momentum. Or study *Book 4—Serving Like Jesus: Six Sessions on Ministry* in late winter to prepare for the spring break missions trip.

Use your imagination and celebrate the completion of each book. Have a worship service, an outreach party, a service project, a fun night out, a meet-the-family dinner, or whatever else you can dream up.

Number of Weeks	Meeting Topic
1	Planning meeting—a casual gathering to get acquainted, discuss expectations, and refine the covenant (page 18).
6	Beginning in Jesus: Six Sessions on the Life of Christ
1	Celebration
6	Connecting in Jesus: Six Sessions on Fellowship
1	Celebration
6	Growing in Jesus: Six Sessions on Discipleship
1	Celebration
6	Serving Like Jesus: Six Sessions on Ministry
1	Celebration
6	Sharing Jesus: Six Sessions on Evangelism
1	Celebration
6	Surrendering to Jesus: Six Sessions on Worship
1	Celebration
2	Christmas Break
1	Easter Break
6	Summer Break

ABOUT THE AUTHORS

A youth ministry veteran of 25 years, **Doug Fields** has authored or co-authored more than 40 books, including *Purpose-Driven® Youth Ministry* and *Your First Two Years in Youth Ministry*. With an M.Div. from Fuller Theological Seminary, Doug is a teaching pastor and pastor to students at Saddleback Church in Southern California and president of Simply Youth Ministry. He and his wife, Cathy, have three children.

Brett Eastman has served as the leader of small groups for both Willow Creek Community Church and Saddleback Church. Brett is now the founder and CEO of LIFETOGETHER, a ministry whose mission is to "transform lives through community." Brett earned his masters of divinity degree from Talbot School of Theology and lives in Southern California.